DATE DUE			
MAR 4 '72			
DEC 11 '72			
GAYLORD			PRINTED IN U.S.A.

ROUSSEAU AND THE
RELIGIOUS QUEST

ROUSSEAU
and the Religious Quest

BY

RONALD GRIMSLEY

PROFESSOR OF FRENCH LANGUAGE AND LITERATURE
IN THE UNIVERSITY OF BRISTOL

CLARENDON PRESS · OXFORD
1968

Oxford University Press, Ely House, London W.1

GLASGOW NEW YORK TORONTO MELBOURNE WELLINGTON
CAPE TOWN SALISBURY IBADAN NAIROBI LUSAKA ADDIS ABABA
BOMBAY CALCUTTA MADRAS KARACHI LAHORE DACCA
KUALA LUMPUR HONG KONG TOKYO

© *Oxford University Press 1968*

*Printed in Great Britain by
The Camelot Press Ltd., London and Southampton*

FOREWORD

This examination of Rousseau's religion is not concerned primarily with its historical origins or influence, these topics having already been the object of detailed treatment by other writers; its main purpose is to examine the essential structure of Rousseau's religious experience, thought, and imagination with a view to bringing out their main values and guiding principles. Because of the considerable development of Rousseau studies in recent decades, it has seemed both useful and opportune to reconsider one of the most fundamental aspects of his life and work.

In view of the modest dimensions of this study, the section devoted to Rousseau's religious thought does not try to follow its gradual development, but treats it as a whole. More detailed comments on the chronological aspect will be found in P.-M. Masson's *La Religion de J.-J. Rousseau* and in the edition of Rousseau's religious writings which, it is hoped, will follow the present volume.

I am grateful to Miss Judith Colwill and Miss Rosemary Manfield for their valuable secretarial help.

R. G.

CONTENTS

Abbreviations	viii
Introduction	ix
I Rousseau's Religious Experience	1
1. Genevan Childhood	1
2. Life with Mme. de Warens	5
3. The Parisian Years	13
4. Intellectual Maturity	17
5. After *Émile*	25
II Rousseau's Religious Thought	36
1. The Role of Philosophy	36
2. God and the Universe	52
3. Man's Inner Life	58
4. Natural Religion and Revealed Religion	68
5. Religion and Society	76
III Rousseau's Religious Mythology	87
1. Paradise	87
2. The Gods	107
3. Hell	123
Conclusion	130
Bibliography	143
Index	145

ABBREVIATIONS

All quotations indicated simply by volume and page number are taken from: *Œuvres complètes de Jean-Jacques Rousseau*, ed. B. Gagnebin and M. Raymond, Bibliothèque de la Pléiade, 1959–. (In course of publication.)

Œuvres	*Œuvres complètes de J.-J. Rousseau*, 13 vols., Hachette, Paris, 1865–70, etc.
CG.	*Correspondance générale de Jean-Jacques Rousseau* ed. T. Dufour and P. P. Plan, 20 vols., Paris, 1924–34.
Corresp. complète	*Correspondance complète de Jean-Jacques Rousseau*, ed. R. A. Leigh, Geneva, 1965–. (In course of publication.)
PF.	La '*Profession de Foi du Vicaire savoyard*' *de Jean-Jacques Rousseau*, critical edition by P.-M. Masson, Fribourg-Paris, 1914.

INTRODUCTION

In Rousseau's opinion, the supreme 'felicity' of religious experience was, like all genuine forms of happiness, ultimately indescribable; any attempt to reduce it to verbal formulae could only distort its true quality by transferring it from the domain of living personal emotion to the cold realm of intellectual abstraction. Although he believed this difficulty to be partly inherent in the nature of language itself, it had been made more acute in modern times by the subservience of language to an insidious 'reflection' that separated man from his 'original' self. In order to prepare the way for a new awareness of human nature, Rousseau insisted upon the necessity of revitalizing both language and experience. As soon as he had been freed from the pernicious effects of a civilized language that was more concerned with expressing false values than with communicating truth about the human condition, man would be able to rediscover the authentic possibilities of his own being.

From the very outset Rousseau insisted that any author who claimed to be working for the good of humanity ought to be personally convinced of the truths he was proclaiming; he considered one of the most serious defects of modern philosophy to be the lack of inner conviction on the part of its propounders. The writer's first obligation was to communicate something of his own being to his work, thereby transforming the language he used into a genuinely personal instrument for the dissemination of sincerely held beliefs; language had to reflect the quality of the experience it was seeking to describe. Only in this way could those to whom it was directed be induced to make an active effort to discover the truth for themselves.

If language pointed beyond itself to the domain of lived experience, the writer's first task was to separate the 'reality' of this original experience from its corrupt and decadent 'appearance' in contemporary society. Thus Rousseau's early works sought to diagnose the malady of civilization, whilst later constructive writings like *Émile* and the *Contrat social* suggested a possible cure; it was first of all necessary to call men's attention to the nature of their predicament before offering them hope of regeneration. He also believed that a vision of regenerated humanity could be presented only by a man who had first discovered it in his own heart. He himself had not found inspiration in a detached observation of the objective world but through an 'illumination' that enabled him to see 'another world' and become 'another man'. 'Whence can the portrayer and apologist of nature, which is today so disfigured and calumnied, have drawn his model if not from his own heart?' (I. 936). Only through 'withdrawing into himself' had he been able to find the 'lost features' of human existence; it was necessary for 'one man' to have portrayed himself in order to reveal the essence of 'primitive man'. Even though Rousseau's didactic writings were concerned primarily with the fate of humanity in general, it was by first of all clarifying the profound possibilities of his own nature that he had found principles capable of guiding the existence of other men.

This subtle interdependence of philosophical and personal experience did not mean that Rousseau was prepared to abandon himself to mere subjective caprice. On the contrary, he constantly stressed that his own personal philosophizing was much more fundamental and universal in its implications than the superficial and insincere reflection of philosophers obsessed with satisfying their own vanity. The reflective bias of modern thought was, in Rousseau's opinion, a characteristic error of the civilization which had mistaken man's intellectual side for his whole being, thus developing reason to the exclusion of morality. In this way the human mind had become the slave of passions and feelings which, in their turn, had been moulded by the corrupting influence of the social process. This did not mean that reason was bad in itself, but that it had to be restored to its proper place in the hierarchy of human values. In other words, even though the genuine thinker admitted his dependence on reason and language, his ultimate concern was with the whole of human experience and not some single part of it.

Rousseau considered these principles to be particularly relevant to any serious discussion of religion. The simplest religious truths were, in his view, the most difficult to attain because their real significance ultimately depended on their appropriation by the individual. When Rousseau's mouth-piece, the Vicaire savoyard, emphasized the anguishing nature of his own search for religious

INTRODUCTION

truth, he was careful to point out that this in no way exempted his 'young friend' from making the same earnest effort to find salvation. Nobody ought to acquiesce passively in another's ideas, however excellent or convincing these might seem to be. 'Je ne veux pas argumenter avec vous, ni même tenter de vous convaincre: il me suffit de vous exposer ce que je pense dans la simplicité de mon cœur. Consultez le vôtre durant mon discours: c'est tout ce que je vous demande.' What finally mattered was not the merely objective meaning of the words used but the active response of the interlocutor to whom they were addressed.

Because of the intimate connexion between experience and philosophy in Rousseau's life and work, any extended discussion of his religion will have to take into account both his personality and his beliefs. The first task of the present study will be to follow the gradual development of Rousseau's religious experience. This does not mean his religious views need be interpreted as a simple 'projection' of personal feelings, because, as we shall see, Rousseau believed that feelings could have objective as well as subjective meaning, but his stress upon the interdependence of personal and philosophical needs makes it necessary to examine the nature of the experience from which the philosophy eventually emerged. I have dealt fairly briefly with the biographical aspect of the problem, for this forms only one aspect of a complex whole. Moreover, any purely chronological treatment of Rousseau's religious development will inevitably be overshadowed by the remarkable work of Pierre-Maurice Masson[1] who favoured this kind of approach, and the first part of this book is indebted to Masson on many points. However, the very substantial amount of research that has been done in the field of Rousseau studies since the publication of *La Religion de J.-J. Rousseau* in 1916 suggests that it may still be useful to reconsider briefly even this well-explored biographical aspect of his religious life, whilst the still more fundamental revaluation of Rousseau's philosophy in recent years, as well as the application of new critical methods to the analysis of his personality, thought, and imagination, have made a

[1] Cf. Pierre-Maurice Masson, *La Religion de J.-J. Rousseau*, 3 vols. (Paris, 1916). The three volumes are: I. *La formation religieuse de Rousseau*; II. *La 'profession de foi' de Jean-Jacques*; III. *Rousseau et la Restauration religieuse*. To this work should be added Masson's invaluable critical edition of the *Profession de foi du Vicaire savoyard de Jean-Jacques Rousseau* (Fribourg and Paris, 1914).

re-examination of his religious outlook seem both desirable and necessary.[1]

Rousseau was the first to acknowledge that any religious viewpoint, however personal its ultimate origin and emphasis, could not be restricted to the idiosyncrasies of individual feeling, but had to be constantly related to principles of universal validity; to give his outlook stability and coherence, the individual had to evolve a philosophy of life and a system of belief that would allow him to transcend the limitations of his own particular situation and draw closer to the life of 'man'. Merely subjective feelings could not provide a satisfactory basis for a permanent religious attitude; the promptings of the heart had to be brought into harmony with the lessons of reason. Even in the personal writings of his last years Rousseau spoke of 'fundamental principles adopted by his reason, confirmed by his heart, and all bearing the stamp of inner assent in the silence of the passions'; he saw his religious philosophy as a 'solid, interconnected body of doctrine' formed with a great deal of 'meditation' and 'care' and 'thoroughly adapted to his reason, his heart and his whole being' (I. 1018).

A close examination of Rousseau's deliberate effort to transform personal intuitions into a coherent system of belief may lead to the conclusion that he subsequently modified his attitude towards the experience—and particularly the emotions—by which they were originally inspired. Masson's failure to give sufficient prominence to this rational factor probably accounts for the exaggerated role he assigns to feeling in his final assessment of Rousseau's religious position. In this respect his systematic exposition and interpretation of Rousseau's philosophy is less satisfactory than his subtle analysis of the religious experience. In order not to confuse the personal and philosophical aspects the present study devotes a separate section to the examination of Rousseau's religious ideas, while naturally admitting their ultimate connexion with his experience.

In spite of their obvious indebtedness to his heart and reason, Rousseau's 'experience' and 'philosophy' probably failed to give adequate expression to the needs of his whole being. In particular, the pressure of idealistic aspirations which could not be satisfied

---

[1] Particularly important are (*inter alios*), Pierre Burgelin, *La Philosophie de l'existence de J.-J. Rousseau* (Paris, 1952), and Jean Starobinski, *Jean-Jacques Rousseau, la transparence et l'obstacle* (Paris, 1957).

through real-life emotion or intellectual achievement induced him to have recourse to an imagination that produced a world of 'beings after his own heart'. Although at its inception this was a predominantly subjective activity inspired by personal fantasies, Rousseau subsequently sought to give shape and substance to his daydreams by making them part of a coherent fictional world expressing some of his most cherished values, and this systematic elaboration of his deepest personal aspirations ultimately involved him in religious issues. To a large extent the spiritual values of *La Nouvelle Héloïse* remained symbolical, since they were not expressed directly, but embodied in particular characters, objects, and situations, the full significance of which the author himself may not have understood. A similar propensity for the indirect symbolical expression of religious values also appeared sporadically in parts of his personal writings. The third section of this essay, therefore, will be devoted to an analysis of what may be called the 'mythological' or imaginative aspect of Rousseau's religion. It is especially to this part of the subject that more recent critical methods, with their emphasis upon the analysis of recurrent themes and images, can be most usefully applied.

Although Rousseau's religious activities were directed upon certain specific and apparently clear-cut issues (the existence of God, the immortality of the soul, the nature of morality, etc.) his 'religion' in the most complete sense of the term was far more complex, for it involved different aspects of his personality and often reflected some of the tensions and contradictions of his life-long striving for self-realization. His religious experience, philosophy, and mythology did not necessarily form a perfectly consistent whole. What he was as a living individual, what he imagined himself to be in moments of despair, exultation, or secret desire, and what he thought should be the universal basis of any valid religious outlook, were not always expressed with the same harmony and clarity, for they involved issues which affected him in different ways. These three aspects of his religious life, with their divergent characteristics, might occasionally appear in the same literary work. Such was the case with *La Nouvelle Héloïse*, which contained a good deal of Rousseau's 'experience' (many details of Saint-Preux's character and situation, at times modified or disguised, were taken from his creator's own life), 'philosophy' (the dying Julie's 'confession of faith' was explicitly identified by

Rousseau with the substance of his *Profession de foi du Vicaire savoyard*), and 'mythology' (the world of Clarens expressed essential aspects of Jean-Jacques's dream of paradise).

In spite of contradictions, these various facets of Rousseau's religious outlook were sustained, as the present study will try to show, by certain common values which helped to give unity to apparently heterogeneous elements. Nevertheless, it would be misleading to limit Rousseau's 'religion' to one specific set of factors, for it was ultimately to be identified with the convergence of them all.

I
ROUSSEAU'S RELIGIOUS EXPERIENCE

1. *Genevan Childhood*

As he looked back in a nostalgic and somewhat idealistic mood upon the events of his early life, the ageing Rousseau was convinced that he had been born into a family noteworthy for its 'piety and morals' and that a 'sound' and 'reasonable' education had merely served to develop the ethical and religious principles of his early environment. A dispassionate examination of the facts would probably modify the details of the picture without impugning its substantial truth. Several relatives had been guilty of moral lapses, of which some, when judged by modern standards, do not appear to have been very grave, although others earned the justifiable reprobation of Genevan moralists: if three aunts (his father's sisters) had created a scandal merely by playing cards after church on Sunday, and Jean-Jacques's mother, Suzanne Bernard, had been severely censured for having 'been present at the theatre, on the Molard, dressed as a peasant-woman', one of his grandfathers, Jacques Bernard, had been accused and found guilty of having seduced two girls, one of whom became pregnant. According to his son, Isaac Rousseau was a 'man of pleasure' who managed to combine enjoyment with 'certain probity and much religion', a *galant homme* in society and a Christian in his 'inner being', but history would lead us to suppose that he was also an irascible, unstable father, who took only a fitful interest in his son's education and eventually left Geneva to escape the legal consequences of a violent quarrel with a retired army officer. However, episodes such as these do not alter the fact that from an early age young Jean-Jacques was influenced by moral and religious values capable of leaving a permanent mark upon his later development.

Historians have pointed out that eighteenth-century Geneva had lost some of the austere Calvinism of the Reformation period, especially in theological matters: liberal thinkers like J. A. Turrettini and Joseph Vernet preferred to stress the moral rather than the doctrinal implications of a Christianity that was becoming increasingly 'reasonable', as it called attention to the 'utility' rather than the 'necessity' of revelation. Although d'Alembert in his *Encyclopédie* article 'Genève' probably exaggerated or misunderstood the Genevan ministers' exact position when he described their religion as 'pure Socinianism' (which meant that they denied the deity of Christ), he rightly called attention to the growing broad-mindedness and even vagueness of their theological outlook. Nevertheless, in questions of moral principle the old rigour persisted, and if Rousseau was probably not subjected to a very strict initiation into religious dogma, he certainly did not escape the strongly ethical, almost theocratic, emphasis of Genevan life. The city elders still considered it their duty to exercise close moral surveillance over their fellow-citizens, constantly exhorting them to righteous living and strict religious observance. If the young people of Geneva no longer went to church with the regularity and enthusiasm of previous generations, they were none the less made aware of the moral and spiritual obligations imposed on them by their membership of the Genevan community. Like most of his young contemporaries, Jean-Jacques attended church services, shared in the singing of psalms from the old Genevan psalter, listened to solemn prayers, Bible-readings and sermons full of moral elevation, and as P.-M. Masson has already pointed out, these childhood experiences left very definite traces in his work.[1] Not only did his style show signs of his assiduous study of the Bible (which he subsequently claimed to have read completely five or six times) and of the tone and movement of Genevan prayers, but in a more general way his whole literary production was reminiscent, in Masson's phrase, of *le sermonnaire genevois*. His later role as one of the leading eighteenth-century moralists was due in no small measure to the ethical environment of his early years.

This Genevan influence may also help to explain another characteristic feature of Rousseau's thought—his refusal to separate the spheres of politics and religion. Genevan citizenship was

[1] Op. cit., I. 30–34. Further valuable information about Rousseau's Genevan background is also given in G. Vallette, *Jean-Jacques Rousseau Genevois* (Paris, 1908). As this section is concerned with biographical problems only in so far as they affect Rousseau's religious development, the reader is referred for further details to existing biographies, especially, F. C. Green, *Jean-Jacques Rousseau* (Cambridge, 1955), and Jean Guéhenno, *Jean-Jacques*, 3 vols. (Paris, 1948–52); English translation entitled *Jean-Jacques Rousseau*, by John and Doreen Weightman, 2 vols. (London, 1966).

synonymous with the acceptance of Christianity, civic and religious activities being simply different aspects of the same fundamental human attitude. The unity of the republic was deemed to depend on the solidarity of its religious outlook, and more especially on its adherence to Protestant Christianity. This Protestant consciousness was also intensified by the knowledge that Geneva was surrounded by powerful Roman Catholic nations whose dangerously close proximity often seemed to threaten the very existence of the small republic. When, therefore, Rousseau introduced the idea of 'civil religion' into the last chapters of his *Contrat social*, he was acting in complete conformity with the religious spirit of his early environment, for this seemed a natural way of securing the political unity of the state.

In the *Confessions* Rousseau does not give many precise details about his early religious upbringing, preferring to dwell upon the almost paradisaic happiness of his childhood. When at the age of eleven he was sent to live with Pastor Lambercier and his sister in the little village of Bossey near Geneva, he enjoyed a blissful existence amid the 'simplicity of rural life'; there he knew the 'pure happiness' of an 'earthly paradise' as it was to be found in a countryside full of a 'sweetness and simplicity that went to the heart' (I. 21). Feeling himself to be the object of his guardians' affection and at the same time his cousin Abraham's true friend and companion, he experienced the type of contentment which was to remain an unforgettable ideal: a life spent beneath the gaze of benevolent, almost divine beings in peaceful, idyllic surroundings. In the *Confessions* Pastor Lambercier and his sister appear as benevolent 'gods' who could 'read' into the pure hearts of Jean-Jacques and his cousin. Only the unfounded accusation of having broken Mademoiselle Lambercier's comb cast a tragic 'veil' upon this 'happy age', by showing for the first time how innocence could be oppressed by injustice and the 'reality' of human goodness destroyed by the 'appearances' of society. Yet Pastor Lambercier, a 'minister full of wisdom and religion', gave him a very favourable idea of the Christian religion by a 'gentle and judicious instruction' which combined practice and precept in a 'discreet and reasonable' way; the minister was 'a very reasonable man' who never asked for the fulfilment of 'extreme' moral obligations. Even formal religious practices seem to have evoked no resistance from Jean-Jacques, who affirms: 'Loin de m'ennuyer au sermon, je n'en sortais jamais sans être intérieurement touché et sans faire des résolutions de bien vivre auxquelles je manquais rarement en y pensant' (I. 62).

On his return to Geneva in the winter of 1724–5 Rousseau was entrusted for a few months to the care of his uncle, Gabriel Bernard. Of his aunt, a devout woman given to 'pietism', he retained a somewhat unfavourable impression, for he later accused her of having paid far more attention to psalm-singing than to the education of her young charges. Moreover, the alacrity with which Gabriel Bernard apprenticed his nephew to an engraver does not suggest any deep avuncular affection, and when his uncle died in 1738, Jean-Jacques affirmed that he had taken 'little care of his wards'. Nevertheless, Rousseau retained a pleasant memory of his sojourn with the Bernards, and in his *Confessions* a few months' stay was prolonged into one lasting two or three years. It was especially the affectionate companionship of his cousin Abraham which made this period of his life so happy, by revealing to him another side of the perfect human existence: an innocent life could be made 'self-sufficient' when it was shared by another human being in a sympathetic environment. His cousin and he were 'always inseparable' and at the same time 'sufficient for each other'. 'Friendship filled our hearts so completely that it was sufficient for us to be together for the simplest tastes to become our delight' (I. 26). This desire to live in an intimate, self-enclosed community represented an ideal which Rousseau was to cherish until the end of his life. In later years he recalled this early period as one in which he had lived in complete harmony with his surroundings.

In spite of his aversion to his aunt's religious habits, Rousseau's attendance at church left a favourable impression upon him, for when his relatives were faced with the problem of training him for a profession, he expressed a preference for the ministry, considering preaching to be 'a fine thing'. Later on he saw himself as an exception to his rule that religion should not be taught to children. 'Find Jean-Jacques Rousseaus at six years of age and speak to them of God at seven; I can guarantee that you run no risk' (I. 62). Unfortunately, when financial considerations forced the family to abandon the idea of a religious calling in favour of apprenticeship to a master engraver, this new phase in his life, far from bringing any spiritual benefit, led to a rapid and catastrophic deterioration of character. By the terms of his contract the young master, Abel Ducommun, was supposed to instruct his apprentice 'in the fear of God and good morals as befitted a family father', but the brutal and apparently worldly bachelor is unlikely to have paid much heed to this obligation.[1] So great became Jean-Jacques's dislike of his new life that he eventually left Geneva on 14 March 1728 to seek his fortune in the world.

2. Life with Mme. de Warens

His almost immediate conversion to Roman Catholicism owed more to youthful opportunism than to religious conviction. In later life he was to feel ashamed of this 'villainous act', and saw himself as a youth who had abandoned the faith of his forefathers for the sake of food and drink. At that time, however, the world of the papists seemed to offer more attractive opportunities for a full and adventurous life than the somewhat restricted environment of Calvinist Geneva. 'Enfant encore et livré à moi-même, alléché par des caresses, séduit par la vanité, leurré par l'espérance, forcé par la nécessité, je me fis catholique, mais je demeurai toujours chrétien' (I. 1013). Recommended by the priest of Confignon to Madame de Warens at Annecy, who in turn sent him to the Hospice for catechumens at Turin, Rousseau apparently made a rapid abjuration of Protestantism, and in April 1728, when he was not quite sixteen years old, was formally received into the Roman Church. Whereas the *Confessions* show us the youthful Jean-Jacques offering a protracted and spirited resistance to the 'frightful idolatry' of his would-be converters, the Hospice records suggest that he abjured in a very short time. Although the length of Rousseau's stay at the Hospice is still unknown, for the records do not give the date of his departure, the ultimate outcome can never have been in doubt. As Masson suggests, the personal decision to become a Roman Catholic had probably been made before his arrival at Turin, and, in any case, owed little to strictly religious considerations. Nevertheless, as Rousseau himself points out, it was only when the doors of the Hospice closed upon him that he fully realized for the first time the gravity of the step he was taking.[2]

[1] Cf. I. 1207-8, for the 'Acte d'entrée en apprentissage de Jean-Jacques Rousseau, 26 avril, 1725'.
[2] Cf. I. 60 f. for Rousseau's account and pp. 1265-6 for the editors' discussion. The exact truth of the matter is still difficult to determine.

More important for his subsequent religious development than any strictly ecclesiastical influence was the person of Madame de Warens, who brought him a new-found sense of emotional fulfilment, 'a perfect confidence' involving 'peace of heart, calmness, serenity, assurance, security'. If he had now left the 'bosom' of his native Geneva, he had discovered an effective substitute in his new protectress. This emotional background is likely to have made adherence to his new religion seem spontaneous and natural. As far as belief was concerned, Madame de Warens may have influenced him in another way: although her own conversion had been largely inspired by the desire to extricate herself from financial embarrassment as well as by the need to satisfy personal pride, her zealous efforts on behalf of the Roman Catholic cause won for her the patronage and financial support of the King of Sardinia and the ecclesiastical authorities. However, this semi-official status and a reputation for piety and good works did not prevent her from adopting an exceedingly ambiguous attitude towards Roman Catholic doctrines: apparently very devout as far as religious practices were concerned, she none the less evolved a private religion of her own which allowed her to reject such fundamental dogmas as original sin and the idea of hell, whilst her whole attitude towards the Incarnation was at the very least extremely vague. Nor does she seem to have felt any misgivings about such a position. In a rather similar way Rousseau himself was later on to reconcile belief in a 'natural' religion with obedience to the national cult, and he too was able to separate what he considered to be the essence of a truly personal religion from its historical Christian form. Even more dubious would appear to have been Madame de Warens's moral outlook, for she had no difficulty in associating religious piety with sexual promiscuity, and through her Jean-Jacques was given his first sexual experience. Thus the very person who helped to secure Rousseau's loyalty to Romanism unwittingly contributed to the weakening of its intellectual and moral hold upon him.

To the religious implications of this deep-seated but complex emotional attachment to a woman older than himself was added the influence of the rural atmosphere in which he was to live for the next few years. His affection for Madame de Warens was often inseparable from his love for nature, of which he had already been given a foretaste during his childhood; describing the idyll of Les

Charmettes, he says: 'Je la voyais partout entre les fleurs et la verdure; ses charmes et ceux du printemps se confondaient à mes yeux.' At such times he had a remarkably expansive sense of personal fulfilment. 'Mon cœur jusqu'alors comprimé se trouvait plus au large dans cet espace et mes soupirs s'exhalaient plus librement parmi ces vergers' (I. 105). Whenever he was able to go for a walk with 'Maman', his heart abandoned itself freely to its feelings. During the memorable Saint-Louis day excursion with her he experienced an extraordinary sense of serenity, the physical world and his own heart being perfectly attuned. The tranquillity and enchantment of the landscape, reinforced by the remarkable purity and translucence of the air and sky, gave him the feeling of living in paradise. Rousseau's most characteristic reactions to nature were thereafter always to contain an important emotional element: the expansive feelings prompted by the sight of the physical world became associated with his reactions to a loved person. At this stage of his life the experience was much too dependent on human feelings to be entirely religious in quality, but it helped to liberate and strengthen emotions from which his religion would ultimately benefit and which even then had specific spiritual overtones.

The prayers he composed during this period reveal a youth uplifted by 'the touching and magnificent spectacle of this vast universe'.[1] No doubt the fervour of these prayers owed more to the impact of natural beauty than to the appeal of the risen Christ, but they were spontaneous and heartfelt. 'Là tout en me promenant je faisais ma prière, qui ne consistait pas en un vain balbutiement de lèvres, mais dans une sincère élévation de cœur à l'auteur de cette aimable nature dont les beautés étaient sous mes yeux. Je n'ai jamais aimé à prier dans la chambre: il me semble que les murs et tous ces petits ouvrages des hommes s'interposent entre Dieu et moi. J'aime à le contempler dans ses œuvres tandis que mon cœur s'élève à lui' (I, 236). The search for immediate emotional satisfaction and the desire to establish direct contact with the source of spiritual power were to be a persistent feature of Rousseau's later religious outlook.

This 'sojourn of happiness and innocence' was a particularly propitious setting for the development of such an aspiration.

[1] The prayers have been published by T. Dufour in the *Annales de la Société Jean-Jacques Rousseau*, I (1905), 221–9.

Henceforth true 'felicity' was to become inseparable from a deepening of present experience, an enhanced feeling of timeless, immediate fulfilment which excluded all regret for the past or anxiety about the future; at such moments Rousseau lived in a kind of eternal present, enriched with 'inexpressible delights' and yet permeated by a kind of 'unchanging tranquillity'; expansion and plenitude combined in a mood that seemed to touch every vital aspect of his inner being.

Nevertheless, it would be wrong to identify his religious experience at this period of his life with the craving for mere emotional satisfaction. In the first place, his Genevan past was too deeply rooted to allow him to be completely forgetful of moral issues. 'Mes prières étaient pures, je puis le dire, et dignes par là d'être exaucées' (I. 236). When he prayed to God, he asked to be kept pure, upright and loyal to moral principles; profoundly conscious of his sins, he felt that the only true pleasures were those enjoyed 'in the exercise of virtue and the practice of one's duties'. Henceforth he would be 'indulgent to others, severe to himself, resist temptations, live in purity, be temperate, moderate in everything and permit himself no pleasures other than those authorized by virtue'. If Rousseau continued to be uplifted by the magnificence and beauty of the vast universe, he was also aware of the moral demands made by religion upon his everyday life.

Moreover, according to his own account, he had already been persuaded to pay attention to the ethical aspect of religion by the example of abbé Gaime, who during his stay at Turin taught him 'the lessons of sound morality and the maxims of right reason' (I. 90–91); abbé Gaime also believed that genuine wisdom must be based on an appreciation of the 'true picture of human life', and that to be happy a man must not be too ambitious, the performance of his daily tasks demanding as much moral effort as the achievement of heroic deeds. So impressed was Rousseau by abbé Gaime's character and attitude that he, along with another priest, abbé Gâtier, later served as a model for the Vicaire savoyard. Yet an influence such as this was not likely to encourage the full acceptance of Christian orthodoxy, since it merely offered him the idea of a 'natural religion' based on moral principles.

If the effect of memory was to transform his stay with Madame de Warens into a time of 'happiness' and 'innocence', his day-to-day life at that time did not always reveal the unity and serenity attributed to it in later years. The self-assertive, even aggressive, elements in his character to some degree resisted this absorption into another's personality, even though it was that of a woman cherished as mother, sister, and mistress. He was too young to have renounced 'all romantic projects' and 'all the follies of ambition'; however great the satisfaction derived from a life that was 'solely occupied with the present', his heart was apt to resist, almost in spite of itself, the lure of this idyllic existence. His belief that he was suffering from a polypus in the heart was probably psychological in origin, and, significantly enough, led to a temporary separation from Madame de Warens when he went to Montpellier to seek a cure for his complaint. With Madame de Warens he suffered obscurely from 'cet ennui de bien-être qui fait pour ainsi dire extravaguer la sensibilité' (I. 247).

Perhaps, too, his life with her was accompanied by a vague feeling of guilt, for, even at the physical level, Rousseau had offered some inner resistance to the intimate side of a relationship which he described as almost incestuous. Already at Turin he had had a more specific experience of wrong-doing when he had allowed a servant-girl to be unjustly accused of the theft of a ribbon which he had actually stolen himself. No longer was he a 'righter of wrongs', but the instrument of injustice, the accuser of the innocent. Even though he later attributed this action to a momentary aberration rather than to any positive desire to do harm, he was to feel a deep and persistent sense of remorse for what he had done. Only by making a public confession of his guilt was he able to find a partial sense of absolution for his wrong-doing.

Constantly fascinated by the ideal of purity and innocence in a timeless idyllic setting, Rousseau could never still the voice of conscience which so often took the form of an anxious reflection upon the implications of his divided inner existence. At the very time when he was enjoying 'a quiet, innocent life' with Madame de Warens he became suddenly obsessed with the problem of evil and damnation, largely, it would seem, as a result of his reading of Jansenist works. Their 'frightening doctrine' filled him with a 'cruel uncertainty', and for a short time he was tormented by the thought of hell. With an ironical sense of his own absurdity, Rousseau describes in the *Confessions* how he banished this fear from his heart: he decided to settle the problem by throwing a stone against a tree; if he hit the tree, he would be saved, if he missed, he would be damned. At the same time he took the precaution of aiming at the broadest tree possible! 'Since then', he affirms, 'I have never doubted my salvation.' Rousseau thus expelled from his mind the question of eternal punishment and even though he could not thereby free himself from all sense of personal guilt, this feeling was to manifest itself in devious and symbolic ways, and only rarely became a direct problem for his immediate consciousness. His characteristic reaction was to identify himself with a feeling or conviction that banished all inner conflict and restored the unity of his personal life.

Rousseau was not content to abandon himself to emotional and moral impulses, for this period was also noteworthy for a protracted and earnest attempt at self-education. For the first time he strove to lay the foundations of a systematic view of human existence. Both his inner life and its outward circumstances led him to work out a philosophy which satisfied intellectual as well as moral and spiritual needs. As he was to put it in his last work, 'la méditation dans la retraite, l'étude de la nature, la contemplation de l'univers forcent un solitaire à s'élancer incessamment vers l'auteur des choses et à chercher avec une douce inquiétude la fin de tout ce qu'il voit et la cause de tout ce qu'il sent' (I. 1014). 'Meditation', 'study', and 'contemplation', all inclined him to view existence in the same purposive, religious manner. Showing at the outset a marked preference for books which combined piety with science, he took as his guide a work well known to his contemporaries and admirably suited to this kind of requirement—Father Bernard Lamy's *Entretiens sur les Sciences* (1683).[1] Lamy constantly stressed the idea that knowledge was important only if it led to a deeper awareness of moral and religious truths. The same attitude was expressed in one of Rousseau's letters to his father: he sought through study 'to train his heart for wisdom and virtue'.[2] This was a viewpoint that he always found very congenial, since he had little interest in purely objective or disinterested forms of knowledge; in religious matters especially he concentrated on what was of 'interest' to him. Similar in emphasis were three other works which he also studied at this time—abbé Pluche's very popular *Spectacle*

---

[1] The subject of Rousseau's intellectual education is discussed by P.-M. Masson in an excellent chapter, 'L'autodidacte et son "magasin d'idées"', op. cit., I. 83–129.
[2] *Corresp. complète*, I. 31.

de la Nature, which combined science and theology in a way that redounded to the glory of God and man, Saint-Aubin's *Traité de l'opinion* (1733) and Le Maître de Claville's *Traité du vrai mérite de l'homme* (1734), which also considered knowledge of the universe from the same moral and religious point of view; according to these works, learning was valuable only when it edified, and in the long run the heart could be more helpful to man than abstract reason. At the more strictly philosophical level Rousseau appears to have been particularly impressed by the English deist, Samuel Clarke, who was to receive fulsome praise in the *Profession de foi du Vicaire savoyard*. As Masson aptly puts it, Clarke was 'Rousseau's metaphysician', for he guaranteed the rational basis of a simplified natural religion based on the existence of a Supreme Being, the separation of mind and matter, the autonomy of human freedom, and the immortality of the soul.

These personal studies thus confirmed Rousseau's acceptance of a religious view of the world by giving his beliefs an apparently serious intellectual basis. If his sensibility already induced him to treat the universal system as the unified and harmonious expression of God's handiwork, his mind henceforth brought rational support to this attitude. At the same time his admiration for the power and intelligence of nature as a universal force made him realize that the things which brought men together were more important than those which kept them apart, and that, consequently, the universal principles of practical morality were more relevant to the welfare of his fellow men than the doctrines of any revealed religion. The long letter of 17 January 1742 on the subject of Pope's *Essay on Man* already suggests that Rousseau's concern with morality easily outweighed his interest in theology.[1] The multifarious and heterogeneous authors studied at this time were also likely to have weakened his attachment to a specific doctrinal standpoint, so that his formal adherence to Roman Catholicism may have been gradually undermined by the results of his researches. Moreover, from the very first Rousseau laid great stress upon the personal relevance of what he read; the desire to achieve a harmonious and balanced view of the physical world was accompanied by an equally urgent need to strengthen his inner life and commit himself to a viewpoint that would bring him stability and peace by protecting him against all the hazards and uncertainties of daily life. His

[1] *Corresp. complète*, I. 132–43. The letter was first published in 1962.

intention was to acquire enough knowledge to be 'self-sufficient and to think without the help of other people' (I. 237). The phrase 'self-sufficient' is a particularly significant indication of the strongly personal emphasis of his studies.

Whatever may have been the ultimate effect of these autodidactic efforts upon his attitude towards Christianity, his relations with many of the ecclesiastics by whom Madame de Warens was constantly surrounded do not suggest that he desired to make any overt protest against his new religion. With certain of them he was on friendly and even affectionate terms, and whenever he was away from Chambéry, he would not forget to pay his respects to 'les Révérends Pères Jésuites'. In short, there seems no reason to doubt his statement in the *Confessions* that he was 'sincerely attached to his new religion'. Although he showed a strong repugnance to bigotry and fanaticism and a dislike of merely outward piety,[1] he carried out his religious observances without difficulty and, significantly enough, does not seem to have raised any objection to the idea of being trained for the priesthood, the ultimate failure of the project being due to his mentors' unfavourable opinion of his suitability rather than to any specific reluctance on his part. For the second time in his life he had come close to an ecclesiastical vocation.[2]

Meanwhile, a more promising career seemed about to open up for him. He had already shown a great fondness for music during his early years. Almost immediately after his conversion, while he was still at Turin, his 'passion for music' had been the main reason for his regular attendance at *la messe du roi*, and later on, when he became secretary to the French ambassador at Venice, he was to show the same enthusiasm for Italian opera and the sacred music of the *Scuole*. His benefactors now proposed to give him a more systematic musical training, and since this was to take place under ecclesiastical auspices, it is likely to have strengthened his attachment to the aesthetic aspects of Roman Catholicism.

---

[1] Cf. Rousseau's letter of May-June 1731 to Esther Giraud in which he says: 'Ma religion est profondément gravée dans mon âme et rien n'est capable de l'en effacer.... Je n'aime pas prôner des dehors de piété qui souvent trompent les yeux et ont de tout autres motifs que ceux que montrent les apparences.' In a letter to his father (?1735) he speaks of 'ce tas de fanatiques et pédants chez qui un faux zèle de religion étouffe tous sentiments d'honneur et d'équité et qui placent honnêtement avec les cartouchiens tous ceux qui ont le malheur de n'être pas de leur sentiment dans la manière de servir Dieu' (*Corresp. complète*, I. 9; 24–25).
[2] Cf., *supra*, p. 4.

3. The Parisian Years

In spite of these various religious influences, Rousseau's arrival in Paris in 1742 and his subsequent friendship with the *philosophes*, as well as the personal difficulties in which he became involved (not least his liaison with Thérèse Levasseur and the abandonment of his five illegitimate children to a Foundlings' home), undoubtedly hastened the disintegration of orthodox religious beliefs. Already his short stay at Lyons in 1740 had probably had an unsettling effect upon his religious life. The 1742 letter on Pope's *Essay on Man* shows that Rousseau favoured morality at the expense of revealed religion, for Pope was praised for having found in 'virtue' and 'peace of heart' the 'true source of happiness'. The Parisian phase probably accelerated a movement which had already begun before his arrival in the capital. In any case, we have already observed Rousseau's tendency to submit himself to his environment and to let his opinions and behaviour be determined by those around him. No doubt his inner life was often less deeply affected than appearances suggested and many old feelings and beliefs continued to slumber undisturbed beneath the changing surface of his conscious reactions, but since his conversion to Roman Catholicism had not been accompanied by any profound spiritual change, his gradual detachment from it became all the easier. As Masson suggests, it is likely that conventional religious practice and belief were completely extinguished by 1747–8.[1] His desire for the 'glory' of Parisian life and an ambitious need to find success in this new environment, his admiration for certain aspects of contemporary taste and the influence of a powerful 'Aristarchus' like Diderot, rapidly removed his dwindling sympathy for Christian orthodoxy and even at times induced him to adopt an aggressively anti-clerical attitude. His interest in the rational and moral aspects of human behaviour led him to reject anything that savoured of 'revelation'. The following remarks to an ecclesiastical correspondent at this time give a typical indication of his mood: 'Je consens que vous leur appreniez toutes les balivernes du cathéchisme, pourvu que vous leur appreniez aussi à croire en Dieu et à aimer la vertu. Faites-en des chrétiens, puisqu'il le faut, mais n'oubliez pas le devoir plus indispensable d'en faire d'honnêtes gens.'[2]

Nevertheless, if friends like Diderot and d'Holbach succeeded

[1] Op. cit., I. 150.   [2] *Corresp. complète*, I. 183.

in arousing anti-clerical feelings and encouraging hostility to traditional Christian dogmas, they could not make him repudiate his belief in God. In his own words, he was 'shaken' but not 'convinced', 'disturbed' but not 'persuaded'. Unable to challenge the *philosophes* with their own intellectual weapons—'I did not know how to combat them, but I did not want to believe them', he was to tell Pastor Vernes in 1758 (*CG*. III. 287)—he would from time to time make an explosive affirmation of his religious principles. Such was the case at the famous dinner given by Mademoiselle Quinault; shocked by the blatantly irreligious tone of the conversation, Rousseau, it is said, threatened to leave if any further insults were offered to his 'friend' God. Although he remained for a long time a prey to doubt and uncertainty and could not help being fascinated by the brilliance of his new cultural environment, he still clung tenaciously, if at times desperately, to childhood beliefs for which he could not at that moment find any adequate rational support.

The famous 'illumination' on the road to Vincennes cannot be treated as a strictly religious experience, in spite of the apocalyptic language with which Rousseau was later to describe it, but it had decisive repercussions upon his subsequent religious development. No longer in doubt about the radical opposition between the true nature of man and the moral decadence of contemporary society, he was soon led to contrast the luxurious corruption of modern life with the happy innocence of the past. Not only did he recall with a certain nostalgic satisfaction the 'simplicity of early times' when men were content to have the gods as 'witnesses of their actions'— a situation not dissimilar from the idyllic bliss of his own early childhood, at least as he was to remember it in his last years—but he also found more precise instances of heroic virtue in ancient states like Sparta and republican Rome; to these historical examples he hastened to add that of his native Switzerland, 'this rural nation' or, as he was to describe it in *La Nouvelle Héloïse*, 'a free and simple country in which one finds ancient men in modern times'. In a word, Rousseau's growing sense of isolation from contemporary society and his consciousness of the tension between his inner self and the requirements of social life induced him to turn back to ancient moral values capable of protecting mankind against the artificiality and decadence of modern civilization; he began to think of Geneva not only as a source of moral strength but also as a remarkable example of purity and innocence in a modern setting. Morality and patriotism tended to coalesce in the same semi-heroic image.

Far from being inspired by any profound religious need, his formal request in 1754 to be readmitted to the Genevan Church was largely due to 'patriotic zeal'. 'Honteux d'être exclus de mes droits de citoyen par la profession d'un autre culte que celui de mes pères, je résolus de reprendre ouvertement ce dernier.' (I. 392). By resuming Genevan citizenship he could affirm his solidarity with a community that offered him at least some sense of social and spiritual kinship. In spite of this public declaration of changed religious loyalties he still accepted one important lesson of 'philosophy', to which he had always been sympathetic,—that religion did not consist of 'this jumble of set phrases' by which many men so often concealed their lack of genuine spirituality. Of themselves, he was now convinced, religious practices were of no great significance: what really mattered was their moral and social function; religious dogma was important only for its human content. At the same time, he recognized that every man had particular attachments too, even in religious matters, not the least of these being his ties with his native land. Since Rousseau believed that specific religious habits were important mainly for their civil or public effect, 'all that was outward form and discipline fell, in each country, within the competence of the laws'; in other words, the ruler had the right to fix the form of the national cult and demand outward obedience to it. A loyal citizen should have no hesitation in accepting the religion of the country to which he belonged. More especially, Jean-Jacques felt that it was his own personal duty to affirm his loyalty to the religion of his forefathers, and he knew in any case that it was impossible to rejoin the Genevan community without being first readmitted to its Church. Furthermore, the formal resumption of Protestantism was not completely unexpected, for he had already begun to prepare the way for this by attending services at the residence of the Dutch ambassador. Finally, the return to his native Geneva had deep personal significance too, as Masson rightly observes,[1] for the re-affirmation of his Genevan origins meant a resumption of childhood values, with all their simplicity, innocence and purity; by becoming a Genevan once more he hoped to purge himself of the

[1] Op. cit., I. 138 f.

corruption to which he had been constantly exposed during his Parisian years.

As a public expression of his renewed devotion to old ideals he dedicated in 1755 the *Discours sur l'origine de l'inégalité* to the Genevan republic. This fulsome eulogy of Geneva was composed by a man who declared that his most cherished ambition was to live 'in quiet fellowship with his fellow-citizens, exercising, in accordance with their example, humanity, friendship, and every other virtue, and leaving behind him the honourable memory of a good man and an honest and virtuous patriot'. Nor did he forget to include in his Preface a somewhat idealized portrait of his father, 'living through the work of his hands and nourishing his soul on the most sublime virtues', with copies of Tacitus, Plutarch, and Grotius interspersed among the tools of his trade. 'By his side I see a dear son receiving with too little profit the affectionate instruction of the best of fathers' (III. 118). Even though religion did not play a prominent part in the *Dédicace*, emphasis being laid on morality rather than on religion as such, Rousseau paid eloquent homage to the ministers, 'those zealous trustees of the sacred dogmas authorized by the laws, those venerable shepherds of souls, whose sweet and lively eloquence all the more readily instilled the Gospel's maxims into the heart because they always began by putting them into practice themselves!' Although everybody acknowledged the fine achievements of *le grand art de la Chaire* at Geneva, 'few people knew to what extent the spirit of Christianity, saintly ways, self-discipline, and gentleness towards others, prevailed among the body of ministers' (III. 119).

Although the content of the *Discours sur l'inégalité* itself was not specifically Genevan, the circumstances of its composition already revealed Rousseau's growing dissatisfaction with contemporary life. To some extent, it is true, Parisian culture still left him inwardly divided, but he was becoming increasingly aware of its harmful effects upon his personal attitude, even though he was still fascinated by its apparent brilliance. Whenever possible, he would make excursions into the surrounding countryside in order to look for some means of renewing his spiritual and emotional resources. To be truly inspired, whether on the literary or religious plane, he had to feel himself close to physical nature, and according to his own account, the fervour of the *Discours* owed much to the natural setting amidst which it was composed; in the forest of

Saint-Germain, where he enjoyed 'one of the pleasantest outings of his life', he was able to find 'the image of early times'. His inspiration assumed an ecstatic, almost religious, quality. 'My soul, uplifted by these sublime contemplations, ascended to the divinity' (I. 388). He understood more clearly than ever before the monstrous error of a contemporary attitude that attributed to nature all the evils perpetrated by man alone.

Nevertheless, the return to Genevan Protestantism indicated no willingness to sever ties with Paris. On the contrary, Rousseau did not seriously consider living permanently in Geneva. Apart from being reluctant to leave his French friends, he doubted whether he could earn an adequate living in his native city; disturbing, too, was the thought that residence in Geneva might involve dangerously close contact with Voltaire. Even so, he realized the difficulty of continuing to live in Paris, a city whose values were so obviously at variance with his own professed ideals. When, therefore, in 1756 his wealthy friend Madame d'Epinay offered him the use of a small country house, 'The Hermitage', he was immediately attracted by the possibility of finding true happiness in a life that reconciled personal inclination and moral conviction. Moreover, he was provided with a wonderful opportunity of completing his literary mission. Instead of having to be content with occasional 'lonely walks' he would henceforth be able to indulge in his feeling for nature whenever he wanted, leading a 'happy, durable life' that would bring to proper fruition the many ideas in his mind. Apparently freed from serious inner contradiction by means of a physical and moral 'reform' which put his life and principles in accord with each other, he was ready to indulge in those expansive feelings which had been stifled by life in the capital. Characteristically enough, as soon as he reached his new home, his first step was to 'deliver himself to the impression of the rural objects by which he was surrounded' (I. 403). He suddenly felt himself transported by *un véritable délire champêtre*. All seemed set for a long period of satisfying creative activity from which his spiritual life would be likely to derive considerable benefit.

4. Intellectual Maturity

The opportunity for a serious re-appraisal of his religious outlook was provided in 1756 by a reading of Voltaire's poems, *Sur le désastre de Lisbonne* and *Sur la loi naturelle*, which prompted him to send the author a very long letter on the subject of 'Providence'. This letter shows very clearly the co-existence of deep personal needs and an effort to give systematic formulation to religious ideas. The work began and ended with a declaration of personal sentiments, although its main sections remained philosophical in character. If Rousseau supported the optimism of Pope and Leibniz,[1] it was because it consoled him in the midst of those very sufferings which Voltaire rejected as unworthy of the human condition. Whereas Pope's poem eased his pain, Voltaire's merely aggravated it by making him discontented with his lot and urging him to bitter protest. Yet Rousseau realized that the existence of suffering compelled him to make a definite choice between hope and despair. The decisive factor in any metaphysical discussion, therefore, was not the intellectual reasoning but its effect upon a man's personal life. It is not necessary to consider at this point the purely philosophical argument, which first concentrated on an obstinate defence of the feeling of human existence as valuable for its own sake (he praised 'the pleasant feeling of existence independent of any other sensation'), and then went on to examine the notion of 'order' within the context of God's existence and its relationship to the universe as a whole. The overriding beneficence of Providence, concluded Rousseau, far outweighed the effect of particular ills, many of which were due to man's own folly and ignorance. At the end of his letter Rousseau again returned to his personal situation as he defiantly opposed the needs of his inner life to the hair-splitting arguments of professional philosophers. Suffering, not empty ratiocination, made a man aware of the true nature of his beliefs. 'Non, j'ai trop souffert dans cette vie pour n'en pas attendre une autre. Toutes les subtilités de la métaphysique ne me feront pas douter un moment de l'immortalité de l'âme; je la sens, je la crois, je la veux, je l'espère, je la défendrai jusqu'à mon dernier soupir, et ce sera, de toutes les disputes que j'aurai soutenues, la seule où mon intérêt ne sera pas oublié.'[2] Thus did will and feeling resolve an issue which mere reason transformed into a process of endless and indecisive reflection.

The religious theme makes only a brief and apparently reluctant

---

[1] Rousseau had already interested himself in Pope's work in 1742. Cf. *supra*, p. 11.
[2] *Corresp. complète*, IV. 81.

appearance in the *Lettre à d'Alembert sur les spectacles* of 1758, the author being obviously disinclined to engage in what he calls 'odious theological disputes'. Although the place accorded in d'Alembert's article 'Genève' to the subject of Genevan religion, and, more especially, the accusation of 'Socinianism' levelled against the clergy, made it necessary for Rousseau to undertake some defence, however limited, of his compatriots' position, he gave the impression that d'Alembert's comments were tactless and inopportune rather than inaccurate. A man's beliefs, he insisted, were his own affair and outsiders had no right to impute to him ideas which he did not wish to recognize publicly as his own. Rousseau left little doubt of his own rationalist sympathies. 'En général, je suis l'ami de toute religion paisible, où l'on sert l'Être éternel selon la raison qu'il nous a donnée' (ed. Fuchs, p. 13). Throughout his discussion he insisted that reason alone was the ultimate court of appeal, and that even the testimony of the Bible, 'the most sublime of all books', which 'consoled and instructed him every day', had to be examined in the light of reason. Consequently, intolerance ought to be banished from all religious discussions. Particularly obnoxious was 'this craze for making proselytes which seemed to animate unbelievers'. Reason and tolerance obviously went hand in hand. Since it was only actions which could be adequately judged, the wisest attitude was to respect people's personal beliefs and 'let God be judge of their faith'.

The sustained intellectual efforts of this period were accompanied by a recrudescence of 'erotic transports'. His liaison with the illiterate Thérèse had brought him only limited satisfaction, physical rather than emotional, and in any case the presence of her importunate mother, who had accompanied them to their country retreat, made it impossible to establish a genuinely intimate life together. Consequently, he sought to compensate for the mediocrity of his own personal relationships by taking refuge in a world of private fantasy where he enjoyed the perfect companionship of 'beings after his own heart'. With the entry of Madame d'Houdetot into his life in 1757 the lonely dreaming which had been responsible for the composition of the first part of *La Nouvelle Héloïse* was suddenly transformed into a tragi-comedy that brought great emotional distress in its wake. The growing embitterment of his relations with friends like Diderot and Grimm served only to increase his inner turmoil, and finally produced disturbing signs of abnormal psychological stress. A period of his life that had begun as a rural idyll was to end in violent quarrels and recrimination, and in 1759, after a sojourn of three years, Rousseau forsook 'The Hermitage' for another home offered by a new protector, the Maréchal de Luxembourg.

As Rousseau's biographers have frequently recounted the detailed events of this period of his life, it will be sufficient to stress here their relevance to his religious experience. The immediate effect of this new situation was to make him acutely conscious of his individual as well as his cultural isolation: he was not merely a man who opposed the false values of his age, but one who believed that he had been betrayed by perfidious friends. Whether he wished to do so or not, he was forced to take stock of his personal position as well as of his philosophical principles; loneliness made him more and more conscious of the need to fortify his inner life against the acute anxiety which now assailed him, almost in spite of himself. Frequent attacks of urinary retention, with their attendant physical suffering, served only to increase his distress. A still more disturbing factor was a persistent feeling of guilt and unworthiness. To some extent Rousseau's emotional difficulties originated in a much earlier period of his existence and probably went back to his childhood years,[1] but even his recent life had been marked by events which were to produce feelings of shame and personal inadequacy. As long as he had been friendly with the *philosophes*, the abandonment of his five illegitimate children to a Foundlings' Home had not aroused any serious misgivings, for he claimed to be merely following the custom of the day; but when he began to look within himself for moral guidance and consult the 'inner voice' by which he henceforth set so much store, he realized that he could not be absolved from blame. In fact, his sense of guilt may have been one of the reasons why he remained with Thérèse in spite of their lack of genuine personal understanding. His remorse became so acute that, when he believed himself to be dying in 1761, he asked his friend, the Maréchale de Luxembourg, to try to find his children. In addition to this disquieting memory, Rousseau was also aware that his moral reputation had been further tarnished by his passion for

---

[1] An account of Rousseau's psychological development is given in my *Jean-Jacques Rousseau: A Study in Self-Awareness*. (Cardiff, 1961.)

Madame d'Houdetot, which had involved him in disloyalty and deceit. This increasing tension, therefore, made it imperative for him to seek for moral and spiritual means of restoring his self-respect. At the same time, his intellectual as well as his personal estrangement from Diderot and the *philosophes* induced him to undertake a systematic clarification of his whole attitude towards religion and morality.

Although *La Nouvelle Héloïse* had begun as a personal fantasy, it tended to become increasingly moral and didactic in its later sections, the final part dealing specifically with the religious question. Indeed, Rousseau later saw his work as an attempt to reconcile the conflicting claims of religious orthodoxy and philosophical scepticism; by making Julie's piety a 'lesson for the philosophers' and Wolmar's atheism 'one for the intolerant', he wanted to show that religion could be lovable and scepticism moral. The main religious emphasis, however, lay in the renewal of Julie's personal existence, which began with the 'inner revolution' experienced on the occasion of her marriage to Wolmar; as the novel developed, increasing importance was attached to the delineation of her spiritual outlook. The dying Julie's 'profession of faith' also provided Rousseau with an opportunity of presenting a summary of his own religious beliefs; and this led directly, as he himself points out in the *Confessions*, to the composition of the *Profession de foi du Vicaire savoyard* included in the fourth book of *Émile*.

Meanwhile, in November 1757 he had tried to put his relationship with Madame d'Houdetot on a more elevated plane by composing for her a series of *Lettres morales*, which also presented, though in a summary and undeveloped form, some of his essential ideas on religion and morality. Rousseau's main intention was to lay down the conditions of a happy human existence, but in the fifth and sixth letters he made it clear that, in his view, complete happiness was impossible without religion. In any serious search for personal values man's primary duty was to look for guidance within himself rather than the outside world. He should 'withdraw into himself' and examine the direction of his 'natural inclinations'. 'Commençons par redevenir nous, par nous concentrer en nous, par circonscrire notre âme des mêmes bornes que la nature a données à notre être; commençons en un mot par nous rassembler où nous sommes, afin qu'en cherchant à nous connaître, tout ce qui nous compose vienne à la fois se présenter à nous.'[1] This in turn would eventually lead to a rediscovery of personal being as well as the re-establishment of a more harmonious relationship with the physical world, the reality of which contrasted so strikingly with the artificiality of 'society'. Friendly solitude in the country, not a busy and anxious social life, was the environment most conducive to the attainment of true happiness. As Rousseau acknowledged at the beginning of the letters, he was writing as much for himself as for his correspondent, and it was his own 'profession de foi' as well as her moral edification that he had in mind.

Parts of the *Lettres morales* were to be incorporated into the *Profession de foi du Vicaire savoyard*, the work in which Rousseau finally defined his religious views. The *Rêveries du Promeneur solitaire* give a brief but vivid account of the personal moral development which led to the completion of his religious testament. Above all else he wanted to settle the moral and religious basis of his existence in a way that would eliminate any further need to return to the examination of its essential principles; he was determined to dispel the tormenting doubt and soul-searching which he found increasingly unbearable. Moreover, with the publication of *Émile* he proposed to end his literary career and 'to contain himself for the rest of his days within the narrow, peaceful sphere for which he was born' (I. 515). It was thus appropriate that his last great didactic work should contain an extended statement of his religious beliefs. After its publication he intended his literary activity to be of a purely personal kind—the composition of 'memoirs' which he envisaged as a work of 'unexampled veracity' and a unique description of a man as he truly was.

Rousseau's retrospective account of this phase of his religious life laid great stress on the interdependence of philosophical and personal factors. Even though he sought to establish rationally valid beliefs, these had to be capable of satisfying the inner needs of one who had always sought 'to know the nature and destination of his being with more interest and care than he had found in any other man'. Purely disinterested knowledge had never had much attraction for Rousseau, as we have already seen, and now that he was dealing with questions which affected the ultimate basis of his

---

[1] *CG*. III. 369. The full text of the 'letters' is to be found in III. 345–74.

existence, the urgency of the issue became overwhelming. He certainly hoped to show other men the way to spiritual salvation, but this could be done only through the clarification and resolution of his own religious problem. He felt that he had passed through a long and tormented phase of his existence, in which he had been frequently torn between the allurements of society and a persistent refusal, perhaps inability, to accept it as it was. He at last realized that although he had allowed himself to be carried along by its 'torrent', he had never been really sympathetic to its essential values. At first he had merely felt isolated from his environment without being able to establish his inner life on a firm basis, so that the years which found him 'hovering' uncertainly between 'prosperity' and 'indigence' also left him divided between 'wisdom' and 'folly'. Henceforth there could be no wavering or compromise; it was imperative for him to establish the real basis of his existence.

The famous reform of the 1750s, in both its physical and moral aspects, had provided him with the opportunity of undertaking a 'severe examination' of his 'inner being' and so of enabling him to 'control it for the rest of his life'. He experienced 'a great revolution' within himself and perceived 'another moral world' from which his fellow men were separated by their 'mad judgements'. His task became all the more important when he recalled the disturbing influence of his philosopher-friends who, far from 'removing his doubts and settling his irresolution', had 'shaken' those beliefs which 'it was important for him to know' without putting anything satisfactory in their place. Unwilling to adopt the 'disheartening doctrines' of the atheists, he had remained inwardly unsettled, whilst his apparent inability to offer any rational and coherent answer to their arguments made it all the more essential for him to resolve his difficulties and establish his intellectual and moral life on a solid basis. He knew that he could never adopt 'a fixed rule of conduct for the rest of his days' until this crucial question of religious belief had been adequately answered. Physical, intellectual, and moral conditions thus had to be reconciled in a single consistent attitude; the 'external and material reform' had to be accompanied by an 'intellectual and moral' reform. 'Fixons une bonne fois mes opinions, mes principes, et soyons pour le reste de ma vie ce que j'aurai trouvé devoir être après y avoir bien pensé' (I. 1016). He was determined to elaborate a system of belief which would satisfy him morally and mentally.

'Il importe d'avoir un sentiment pour soi, et de le choisir avec toute la maturité de jugement qu'on y peut mettre' (I. 1018). It was not enough for him to have broken with what he considered to be false friends and pernicious principles; he had also to justify this drastic step by seeing it in the light of a carefully pondered view of existence as a whole.

The various stages through which the *Profession de foi* passed before attaining its final form prove that Rousseau, far from finding an immediate solution to the religious problem, carried out his intentions, as he put it, 'slowly and sporadically'. Moreover, some parts of this work had already been anticipated, as we have seen, by earlier discussions such as the letter to Voltaire in 1756, the *Lettres morales*, the *Lettre à d'Alembert*, *La Nouvelle Héloïse*, and other briefer pieces. However, it was in the *Profession de foi* that he presented a final synthesis of his beliefs and established principles which he did not thereafter propose ever again to call into question.

His installation at Montmorency in May 1759 and the severing of contact with his former friends had at first augured well for the success of this enterprise. Having finally renounced the 'chimeras of friendship', he felt a wonderful sense of liberation, and wrote the fifth and last book of *Émile* in a 'continual ecstasy'. Every morning he would hasten to greet the sunrise with an extraordinary sense of religious exaltation: an indescribable rapture left him powerless to utter anything but 'O great being! O great being!' At such moments he seemed to recapture the enchantment of an 'earthly paradise', for he enjoyed an extraordinarily vivid feeling of personal innocence.

Unfortunately this new-found happiness was too precarious to dispel all his inner anxiety. Perhaps the very intensity and earnestness of his efforts, as well as a sudden onset of physical suffering, were calculated to create a mood of acute anxiety, which crystallized around the publication of *Émile*. He became convinced that the Jesuits had obtained possession of the manuscript in order to publish it in a mutilated form. If he had enjoyed the friendship of individual Jesuits during his Roman Catholic days with Madame de Warens, he came to see the Society of Jesus as a ruthless, power-ridden organization bent on universal domination; it seemed to him quite natural that they should follow their 'ancient maxim' of 'crushing the wretched' by being hostile to a work which laid such great stress upon the role of freedom. Moreover, to his mental distress was added the severe physical pain caused by a catheter that had broken off in his urethra. The belief that this accident was likely to prove fatal made Rousseau all the more anxious about the destiny of his most important work, the one that expressed the noblest side of his mind and character. It was largely through the sensible exhortations of Malesherbes and other friends that he was eventually persuaded to acknowledge the baselessness of his suspicions.

5. *After* Émile

The publication of *Émile* in 1762 disrupted his life in a still more catastrophic way. The book was condemned by the Paris Parlement and an official order issued for its author's arrest. To escape imprisonment and to avoid compromising those friends who, like the Maréchale de Luxembourg, had been associated with the publication of the work, Rousseau fled from France. Yet in some respects real persecution was mentally less disturbing to Rousseau than imaginary ills, and during his flight he found time to begin the composition of a pastoral poem in prose, a kind of religious idyll, *Le Lévite d'Éphraïm*, which was inspired by his reading of the Bible and a translation of Gessner's *Idylls*. Of only mediocre literary value, this little work was always very dear to Rousseau—'*Le Lévite d'Éphraïm*, if it is not the best of my works, will always be the most cherished' (I. 586)—since it proved his ability to detach himself from the wickedness of the world and find consolation in the 'antique simplicity' and naïve innocence of a patriarchal age; even in the midst of the greatest adversity Rousseau showed that his heart could remain unembittered.

When he eventually found refuge in Môtiers-Travers in the principality of Neuchâtel, which was at that time under the protection of the King of Prussia, Rousseau sought to establish friendly relations with the Protestants of the region, and went so far as to make a declaration of Christian faith to the local minister, M. de Montmollin, with a view to regularizing his relationship with the Protestant Church. At first his gesture was well received and he was able to find great comfort in participating in the Holy Communion. Perhaps the ultimate satisfaction which Rousseau derived from religious observance was human rather than spiritual, for he found consolation in the thought that he was once again sharing life with his 'brethren'. This sense of human solidarity was one of the most significant aspects of his religious life at this time; the feeling of human brotherhood far outweighed any doctrinal difference that may have existed between his beliefs and theirs. 'D'accord avec eux sur les principes de nos devoirs, je ne dispute point sur le reste, qui me paraît très peu important.' If in one sense he was simply performing his 'duty as a citizen', he was also fulfilling himself as a human being, and, more especially, as a lonely, persecuted man who believed that he had at last found sympathy and understanding. 'Toujours vivre isolé sur la terre', he wrote in the *Confessions*, 'me paraissait un destin bien triste, surtout dans l'adversité. Au milieu de tant de proscriptions et de persécutions je trouvais une douceur extrême à pouvoir me dire, au moins je suis parmi mes frères, et j'allai communier avec une émotion de coeur et des larmes d'attendrissement qui étaient peut-être la préparation la plus agréable à Dieu qu'on y pût porter' (I. 605). Intending to 'live and die in the communion of the reformed Christian Church', he hoped henceforth to consider M. de Montmollin as his 'pastor' and the minister's parishioners as his 'brethren'.

The hostility of the Roman Church made friendship with the Protestants all the more consoling, and when he composed a vigorous refutation of the *Mandement* which the Archbishop of Paris had issued against *Émile* on the grounds that it contained 'an abominable doctrine likely to overthrow the natural law and destroy the foundations of the Christian religion', Rousseau undoubtedly hoped to draw still closer to his Protestant friends. The *Lettre à Christophe de Beaumont* was a particularly effective piece of religious polemics, which dealt not only with questions of general principle but also contained an impressive personal apology. He hoped too that the strongly anti-Roman Catholic tone of the work would reassure those fellow-citizens who had been disturbed by the apparently heretical implications of the *Profession de foi*. Not only did he seem to identify himself with the Protestant tradition when he made a vigorous onslaught on the Roman doctrine of transubstantiation, but he also made a particular point of expressing his gratitude to the 'worthy pastor', M. de Montmollin, who had welcomed to his church 'a defender of God's cause'.

All Rousseau's efforts to win over his fellow-Protestants proved unavailing. In vain did he declare himself to be in complete agreement with them on the only thing that mattered—the fulfilment of moral obligations; in vain too did he promise to remain silent on all questions of theological doctrine. Even his proud claim to have been born into the 'holiest and most reasonable of all religions' did not help his case, for political considerations were soon to aggravate the difficulty of the religious issue. The *Contrat social* had angered the ruling Genevan aristocracy by its radical emphasis upon the idea of the sovereignty of the people—a principle not incompatible with the theoretical basis of the Genevan Constitution, but one that was certainly not acceptable to its existing rulers. Rousseau found himself engaged in such acrimonious controversy with those whose cause he had hitherto espoused that on 12 May 1763 he formally renounced his Genevan citizenship. A few months later the *procureur-général*, Jean-Robert Tronchin, attacked Rousseau in his *Lettres écrites de la Campagne*, to which Jean-Jacques replied with a vigorous polemical work entitled *Lettres écrites de la Montagne*. The religious section is interesting chiefly for Rousseau's attempt to define Geneva's position in relation to the main principles of the Reformation; the Genevan ministers were accused of having betrayed those principles and of having become as intolerantly sectarian as the Church they were supposed to be reforming.

The breach became irreparable and in his correspondence Rousseau did not hesitate to express his bitter resentment against the Genevan clergy; he complained of 'the vexatious interference of the priestly rabble' and the contemptible activities of 'these poor little ill-made puppets'; he deplored, too, the dogmatism and intolerance of those who refused all infallibility to the Roman Church in order to usurp it for themselves (*CG*. XV. 139); he regretted particularly the way in which the Genevan clergy had prevented him from enjoying the 'society of his brethren' and participating in this 'simple, pure cult', which was 'precisely what his heart needed'. His resentment against the Protestants became so great that he began to think seriously of settling in a Roman Catholic country. He was tempted to make his peace with all clergy except the Genevan, whom he proposed to transform into 'the scape-goat for the sins of Israel'. In 1765 we find him reminding a correspondent that he had always been on good terms with the Roman Catholic clergy; he recalled his friendly relations with the Oratorians, 'the austere curé of Montmorency' and 'the venerable curé of Groslay'. 'Je n'ai trouvé que des amis dans votre clergé: dans le nôtre, je n'ai trouvé que des furies; les inquisiteurs de Goa sont des agneaux auprès d'eux. Ah! si l'on voulait me laisser mourir en pays catholique' (*CG*. XIII. 86). A little later, when he thought of going to live in Corsica, he even affirmed that he would be willing to attend Mass, as long as this were not taken to mean a change of religion on his part. That this was no thoughtless remark is shown by the reappearance of the same idea a year or two before his death. 'Je n'ai nulle répugnance à aller à la Messe: au contraire dans quelque religion que ce soit, je me croirai toujours avec mes frères, parmi ceux qui s'assemblent pour servir Dieu' (*CG*. XX. 333–4). On this occasion, too, he insisted that this did not imply his formal adherence to Roman Catholicism or the acceptance of some kind of 'dogmatic religion'.

Rousseau allowed himself to make only one more excursion into religious controversy. This took the form of a somewhat ineffectual satirical pamphlet called *La Vision de Pierre de la Montagne dit le Voyant* (1765), which purported to deal with the 'miraculous' aspects of his persecution by the clergy. The following year he severed all contact with the Protestant Church.

In the meantime he had found at Môtiers a new pastime which compensated him in some measure for his growing isolation from other men by bringing him into close touch with the nature he loved so much. Whereas his previous ecstasies had tended to take the form of an identification with the 'system' of nature as a whole, he was now given an opportunity of studying her in detail, for about 1764 his friend, Dr. d'Ivernois, began to interest him in botany. Although this activity was intended primarily as a form of relaxation, it served also to make him aware of another aspect of God's universe by revealing nature's astonishing complexity and 'prodigious variety'. Once again he was impelled to admire the power and wisdom of the Creator, as he examined 'this chain of relations and combinations which overwhelmed the observer's mind with its marvels' (I. 641).

When in 1765, after the 'stoning' at Môtiers, Rousseau decided to leave the region of Neuchâtel, he stayed for a short time on the Île de Saint-Pierre in the Lac de Bienne and there enjoyed an experience of nature that was to provide a unique memory for the rest of his life. He had a sense of incredible rapture as he abandoned himself to a mood of speechless adoration before the beauty of the scene. This was a particularly intense form of an experience which had always given him great satisfaction, for he never failed to feel 'strangely moved' at the sight of a fine landscape. Rarely did he remain insensitive to 'the entrancing sight of nature'. Even though the experience defied verbal or rational description, he knew that it contained a powerful religious element which made him lift up his heart to God in a movement of indescribable ecstasy. He willingly associated his attitude with that of the old woman whose only prayer was 'Oh!' 'This best of all prayers was also his' (I. 642).

As he grew lonelier, Rousseau found in nature a kind of spiritual refuge. We have already seen the important role played by the feeling for nature in the development of his early religious experience; with his increasing aversion to intellectual activity, he gave himself readily to 'these heart-felt feelings which did not involve the fatigue of thinking'. Such a mood was perfectly attuned to the existence of a man who intended henceforth to follow the 'impulse of the moment' and enjoy the fullness of immediate emotional experience. As he wandered alone in the countryside 'out of the reach of the wicked'—and especially when he was fortunate enough to find himself close to a lake—he would abandon himself to his reveries and from time to time exclaim with deep feeling, 'O nature, O mother, here I am under thy sole protection' (I. 644). The same feeling was to reappear in his very last years.

Ecstatic admiration for the beauty of nature was often accompanied by an enhanced awareness of his personal existence. Far from allowing himself to become passively absorbed in a kind of sensuous rapture, Rousseau would sometimes think of himself as another Robinson Crusoe building an 'imaginary dwelling' on a picturesque island where everything seemed capable of satisfying his deepest needs. As the famous fifth Promenade of the *Rêveries* clearly shows, personal consciousness might go beyond the confines of his physical environment. As he explored the depths of his inner being, he would ultimately identify himself with the pure 'feeling of existence', which lifted him above the contradictions and imperfections of everyday existence by making him 'self-sufficient like God'. At such moments he would enjoy an extraordinary feeling of plenitude, a 'full, perfect, and sufficient happiness' which left nothing more to be desired.

Unfortunately for Rousseau the idyll of the Île de Saint-Pierre was short-lived, for he soon received an order to leave the territory of Berne. His subsequent journey to England in 1766 involved him in intense emotional and mental strain and the onset of delusions of persecution. Forced to rely on himself in the midst of what he believed to be a hostile environment, he sought comfort in the study of the Bible, of which he had always been an assiduous reader. He began to copy out passages which he believed to be relevant to his own situation, showing a particular predilection for the prophet Isaiah.[1] Jeremiah was another prophet whose message he found relevant to his own needs; later still he saw a striking analogy between his own situation and that of the persecuted Job. Moreover, his reading was not confined to the Bible, for about 1763 he bought a Latin edition of Thomas à Kempis's *Imitation of Jesus-Christ* which he apparently read with some diligence.[2] According to Bernardin de Saint-Pierre, Rousseau in his last years made 'a little book out of a few pages of the Old and New Testaments, and especially of Ecclesiastes and the Sermon on the Mount, and he would carry this around with him wherever he went'.

Occasionally he could be induced to re-examine or at least re-affirm some of his fundamental ideas. Although he had for a long time treated his *Profession de foi* as a final statement of his religious views, a letter he received in 1769 from a young man called Franquières, who was worried by religious doubts, prompted him to return to the subject. This was in fact to be Rousseau's last attempt to present a brief but systematic summary of his essential religious ideas, even though the religious theme was to recur sporadically in the *Rêveries*. At the end of his letter he told his correspondent: 'Voilà la dernière fois que je reviendrai sur ces matières. J'ai voulu vous complaire, monsieur; je ne m'en repens point: au contraire, je vous remercie de m'avoir fait reprendre un fil d'idées presque effacées, mais dont les restes peuvent avoir pour moi leur usage dans l'état où je suis' (*CG*. XIX. 63).

The gradual darkening of his mind made it increasingly difficult for him to distinguish between real and imagined persecution; the world began to rise up before him in a strangely menacing form. Yet even in moments of greatest anxiety he clung to his faith in

[1] Cf. Masson, op. cit., II. 241, for details of the passages.
[2] Ibid., 243.

Providence, mysterious and alarming though its manifestations sometimes seemed to be: it was often difficult for him to distinguish between the implacable decrees of a cruel 'fatality' and the benevolent protection of a friendly divinity. In Rousseau's eyes power was always enigmatic and usually dangerous; beneficent as long as it was sustained by moral feeling, it could be relentless and destructive when it was reduced to its physical components; he believed that 'injustice always went with power' and 'justice was always in the wrong in relation to power'. He distrusted organized bodies because, in his opinion, power could not admit of error or weakness.

Moreover, if at times of ecstatic identification with the beauty of nature Rousseau felt himself to be very close to God, these were privileged moments, rare and precious, but utterly incapable of offering permanent protection against the hostility of the world. 'Fate' seemed constantly to be directing him away from solitude towards perilous involvement with human beings. In such circumstances his religious faith was still active, but had to struggle with the thought of God's mysterious silence. Apparently deprived of any direct spiritual help, he was confronted with the ambiguous and often frightening world of physical signs, the precise meaning of which had to be interpreted by his anxious and uncertain mind. Everything was now divided between light and darkness, good and evil, with evil as the more constant factor and goodness so apparently ready to transform itself into its opposite. The smiling countenance of a seemingly faithful friend could suddenly change into the 'misshapen, almost hideous face' of a fearsome enemy.[1] On all sides he could detect nothing but the 'frightful signs' of a terrible 'destiny' that wanted him to suffer for the sake of its own inscrutable purposes. Goodness continued to exist no doubt, but for the time being appeared to have taken refuge in the unsullied heart of Jean-Jacques Rousseau.

In moments of greatest stress he still clung tenaciously to the thought of his 'innocence' and 'goodness', which were henceforth endowed with religious significance. He was so firmly convinced of his exceptional position as a persecuted man that he tended to see an analogy between his own cause and that of Jesus. The identification, on which Masson has already commented ironically, was

[1] The expression was used by Rousseau in the course of his quarrel with his friend Du Peyrou in 1767.

a barely conscious one, and probably less shocking in somebody who did not accept the idea of the Incarnation than in an orthodox Christian, but it clearly revealed the nature of Rousseau's later reactions to his desperate situation. More especially, it confirmed his interpretation of life as a struggle between the innocent and the wicked; he was convinced that he himself had been singled out by Providence as a 'martyr' destined to suffer for the 'truth'. The comparison with Jesus, therefore, was simply the culmination of an attitude that had gradually developed over the years until it finally assumed a quasi-religious meaning.

The thought of his innocence made him more and more determined to entrust himself to Providence. 'Je me tais devant les hommes et je remets ma cause entre les mains de Dieu' (*CG.* XVII. 53). 'Await my destiny', 'put my fate in the hands of Providence', such are the expressions used by his conscious mind, but inwardly he was still divided. The idea of 'resignation' was made all the more terrifying by the apparent absence of any overt hostility; he believed he was surrounded by a conspiracy of silence, almost claustrophobic (he spoke of being 'buried alive among the living') in its effects. He was appalled by 'the deep universal silence, not less inconceivable than the mystery it concealed, a mystery which had been hidden from him for fifteen years with indescribable care and with a truly miraculous success' (I. 662). To the silence of men was now added the awesome silence of God Himself. Nevertheless, he refused to abandon his religious faith and as soon as he had completed his *Dialogues*, the work that was to justify him in the eyes of posterity, he treated it as *un dépôt remis à la Providence*. This lonely, persecuted, and unhappy stranger, as he called himself, who placed his only hope in 'eternal Providence', was determined to make one last gesture and then await whatever consequences God had willed for him, sustained by the thought that order would one day be restored to the world.

The failure of his attempt to place the manuscript of the *Dialogues* on the high altar of the cathedral of Notre Dame exposed him once again to 'men's iniquity'. More unfortunately still, he again felt compelled to read the 'signs' he saw around him. The philosopher Condillac's return to Paris was at once interpreted as *une direction de la Providence* which would allow him to lift the 'veil of darkness'. Then, seized with doubt about Condillac's character, he saw in an English visitor, young Brooke Boothby, 'the trustee whom Providence had chosen for him'. In all this he discerned 'the finger of God' pointing to 'the work of Providence' and providing him with the 'certain sign' that his manuscript would be ultimately preserved from destruction. In spite of some misgivings, Rousseau, at last assured that 'Heaven in its turn would do its work' even though he himself did not know the time or the place, gradually achieved some degree of 'resignation'; he drew great comfort from the thought that because 'the essence of his being' was 'ever the same', it could no longer be vulnerable to 'men's looks'. As he considered his position with greater tranquillity, Rousseau began to look beyond the 'barrier of eternity' to a time when men would no longer exist for him and he would be able to enjoy 'eternal happiness'. His 'felicity' would thus be of a kind unknown to ordinary mortals.

Hope of immortality became a constant preoccupation in Rousseau's last years, no longer accepted as a mere 'doctrine' but forming a deeply personal conviction which alone could give meaning to his immediate situation. His hostility to the *philosophes* was now based almost exclusively on the assumption that, as 'missionaries of atheism', they would continue to persecute him for his belief in God; in their determination to enjoy the pleasures of this world they were resentful against anybody who dared to remind them of life in the next. On the other hand, Rousseau believed that it was only in the life after death that a man like himself could be freed from the trammels of this earthly existence, and become a complete self. In this respect the Vicaire savoyard had clearly reflected Rousseau's own views when he affirmed: 'J'aspire au moment où, délivré des entraves du corps, je serai *moi* sans contradiction, sans partage, et n'aurai besoin que de moi pour être heureux' (*PF*. 291–3). If Jean-Jacques longed for this 'state of happiness, strength, and virtue', it was largely because he would then be able to fulfil himself in his immediate reality, 'without division or obstacle'. Religion, and more specifically the belief in immortality, was a constant source of comfort and hope in his last years, for, however desperate his earthly situation might be, he looked forward to the day when he would be delivered from all inner conflict and outward adversity. The perfect felicity to which he so ardently aspired would at last be his.

In his last years Rousseau was continually fascinated by what he considered to be the most impressive feature of the divine being:

God depended on nobody but Himself; He was completely self-sufficient. If God had created finite creatures to be as 'happy, free, and good' as Himself, Rousseau believed that they would enjoy in the next life the incalculable bliss of a self-sufficient existence. Already the pure 'feeling of existence' experienced in the state of reverie had given him a glimpse of the happiness to come.

Some critics have seen in this yearning for God-like self-sufficiency a proof of Rousseau's mental unbalance. Whilst it may be agreed that his attitude leaves a somewhat disturbing impression on a modern reader, it should not be confused with the genuine megalomania in which a true madman believes himself to be God. Although the longing for self-sufficiency undoubtedly expressed Rousseau's desperate effort to protect himself against the idea of universal persecution, it also had the more positive function of enabling him to reach a deeper level of personal experience; the reference to God was probably intended to express a powerful analogy rather than a statement of fact. In any case, this idea did not constitute a single, all-consuming obsession, even as far as religion was concerned, but formed part of a complex pattern of behaviour.[1] To some extent, it is true, the religious outlook of Rousseau's last years reflected the tensions and conflicts of his character, and, as such, it was a religion of mood rather than dogma; being rooted in his own being, his 'natural religion' inevitably contained some highly personal elements. Nevertheless, the subjective aspect of certain characteristic moods did not mean that Rousseau was prepared to repudiate the beliefs expressed in the *Profession de foi du Vicaire savoyard*, beliefs he held to be grounded in his whole being and not some particular part of it. To the very end he held fast to his conviction that all physical existence had its foundation in God and that the 'universal system' ought ultimately to be interpreted as God's handiwork; there was an essential conformity between man's immortal soul and the spiritual reality underlying the structure of the physical universe. If man was able to respond so spontaneously to the beauty of creation, it was because of the link established by God between his spiritual being and the system of which it formed part.

Although the religion of Rousseau's last years remained diffused and varied in its expression, being often determined by the impetus

---

[1] Cf. my *Jean-Jacques Rousseau: A Study in Self-Awareness* (esp. Ch. 8) for a more detailed examination of this point.

of particular moods and circumstances, his persistent desire to fulfil himself as a truly 'natural' man always led him back to what he considered to be the original and ultimate ground of all being. Even in moments of direst need, when all seemed lost, he never abandoned faith in Providence as the power guiding the destiny of man and the world. Everything would in the end return to its proper order, and even the fate of the unfortunate Jean-Jacques would take its appointed place in the universal scheme of things.

According to Thérèse, Rousseau, as he was dying, tried to take a last look at the nature he loved so much, crying out: 'Être des Êtres . . . Dieu! Voyez comme le ciel est pur, il n'y a pas un seul nuage. Ne voyez-vous pas que la porte m'en est ouverte et que Dieu m'attend?'[1] The story may have been Thérèse's own invention, for it would presumably have been difficult for a man struck down by a sudden fit to have the time or energy to utter such words. Be that as it may, it is remarkable that Thérèse's untutored mind should have so faithfully reproduced one of Jean-Jacques's characteristic religious moods; even the reference to the cloudless sky is a curiously authentic reminiscence of his reaction to physical nature. She was, therefore, not being disloyal to his life-long aspirations when, after his death, she wanted him to be known as a man of God.

[1] Cf. F. C. Green, *Jean-Jacques Rousseau* (Cambridge, 1955), p. 358, for further details of the episode.

II

ROUSSEAU'S RELIGIOUS THOUGHT

1. *The Role of Philosophy*

ROUSSEAU'S attempt to give a systematic account of his religious views is very much influenced by his critical attitude towards philosophy in general, and many of his animadversions against contemporary thought are equally applicable to his criticism of orthodox religion. Like most eighteenth-century thinkers he is sceptical of the claims of traditional metaphysics to say anything meaningful about ultimate reality; man is prevented, he believes, by his finite nature and 'the insufficiency of the human mind' from understanding the mystery of the absolute. 'Nous n'avons pas les mesures de cette machine immense, nous n'en pouvons calculer les rapports; nous n'en connaissons ni les premières lois ni la cause finale; nous nous ignorons nous-mêmes. . . . Cependant nous voulons tout pénétrer, tout connaître. La seule chose que nous ne savons point, est d'ignorer ce que nous ne pouvons savoir' (*PF*. 55). In his letter to M. de Franquières in 1769 he insists that 'the contemplation of the infinite will always exceed the limits of my intelligence' (*CG*. XIX. 49). Consequently, the words 'metaphysics' and 'metaphysical' almost invariably have an unfavourable meaning in Rousseau's work. In the *Profession de foi* he speaks of 'metaphysical discussions which are beyond my comprehension and yours, and which ultimately lead to nothing' (*PF*. 263-5), whilst Julie in *La Nouvelle Héloïse* refers contemptuously to 'the darkness of metaphysics' and 'these abysses of metaphysics which have neither bottom nor shore' (II. 699). Since metaphysics has no firm basis in experience, it produces abstract systems which are no more than sterile flights of the imagination. In this respect Rousseau's attitude is not dissimilar to that of Voltaire and other contemporary thinkers who reject philosophical system-building in favour of a return to 'experience'. Even though the interpretation of this term creates further problems and differences, there is widespread agreement about the futility of abstract metaphysics.

THE ROLE OF PHILOSOPHY

Such is Rousseau's distrust of professional philosophizing that he consistently refuses to call himself a 'philosopher'. He undoubtedly associates himself with the view of his mouth-piece, the Savoyard priest, who states: 'Je ne suis pas un grand philosophe, et je me soucie peu de l'être. Mais j'ai quelquefois du bon sens, et j'aime toujours la vérité' (*PF.* 39). Similarly in the *Lettre à M. de Beaumont* he readily agrees with the archbishop's assertion that he is not a 'philosopher'. 'Oh! d'accord, je n'aspirai jamais à ce titre, auquel je reconnais n'avoir aucun droit, et je n'y renonce assurément pas par modestie.' In the same work he does not hesitate to call himself 'the friend of truth'. In his letter to Voltaire on Providence he describes himself—perhaps not without a trace of irony—as 'a friend of truth who speaks to a philosopher'. If he seeks to build a 'system' of belief, it is as 'a simple, truthful man'. Rousseau makes it clear that a genuine love of 'truth' and an enthusiasm for 'philosophy' can be two quite different things!

In a general sense Rousseau's distrust of metaphysics, though owing something to the contemporary philosophical attitude, stems mainly from his critical attitude towards 'society' as a whole. Like other essential forms of human concern, philosophical values have been corrupted by the development of nefarious social influences. The brilliance of contemporary culture, as he already stresses in his first *Discours*, is not a sign of progress but of deterioration; like the bright flush on the cheeks of a stricken man it betokens the presence of an illness that may well prove fatal. The triumph of 'philosophy' means the defeat of 'virtue', for moral values are everywhere being sacrificed to intellectual distinction. Consequently, philosophical and moral attitudes have become so perverted that thinkers can no longer see the real problem that should be engaging their attention: preoccupied with explaining the constitution of the universe, they have forgotten the reality to which all such explanations must ultimately be related—the nature of man himself.

According to Rousseau, this one-sided emphasis on intellectual values unfortunately encourages thinkers to seek philosophical sophistication for its own sake, so that they become hopelessly entangled in problems which have no serious bearing on human experience. Contemporary philosophizing, he says, is simply an excuse for the elaboration of needless 'subtleties', another word constantly used by Rousseau in a pejorative sense. Far from bringing a man closer to the truth, the 'subtleties of metaphysics' merely lead him further astray; the 'vain subtlety of arguments' serves only to induce the unwary thinker into grievous error. It is largely through its preoccupation with 'senseless refinements' that philosophy has proliferated into a multiplicity of conflicting systems which cause ordinary people to lose themselves in the 'huge labyrinth of human opinions'. All too often the philosophers, Rousseau tells Franquières, content themselves with a mere *clinquant de paroles*. 'Jamais le jargon de la métaphysique n'a fait découvrir une seule vérité, et il a rempli la philosophie d'absurdités dont on a honte, sitôt qu'on les dépouille de leurs grands mots.' The pursuit of barren generalities and abstractions is encouraged by this unprofitable playing with words and empty formulas. Inevitably theologians, obsessed with 'the subtleties of vain disputes' and the 'subtle interpretations of dogmas', have become afflicted with the same malady. To this severe criticism of 'subtlety' Rousseau returns again and again in all his writings; his distrust affects his attitude towards morality and aesthetics as well as philosophy and religion. He believes that an exclusive concern with various forms of subtlety betrays not only an inability but a wilful refusal to face the truth. The subtle man, Rousseau avers, is both sophistical and insincere; extreme subtlety is but a convenient way of evading the obligation to seek the truth, both in thought and morals. Rousseau believes, moreover, that as religious dogmas grow in subtlety, so morality steadily declines. 'La doctrine se raffine, et la morale dépérit toujours plus' (*Œuvres*, III. 92). Intellectual refinement and moral decadence thus go hand in hand.

The most disturbing conclusion to be drawn from so many philosophical disputes is that in modern society language has suffered the same deterioration as other forms of human activity. Language has not only become confused and imprecise, but an actual instrument of error. What people say no longer corresponds to what they do or even think. 'Appearance' and 'reality' represent two entirely different kinds of phenomena. Nowhere is this more strikingly obvious than in the sphere of social intercourse, where genuine human obligation is obscured by a cloud of polite verbiage or meaningless jargon. Unfortunately philosophers and theologians are particularly prone to the abuse of language. Rousseau, like Saint-Preux, despises 'this deceptive ostentation which consists only of vain discourse' and 'this futile philosophy which produces mere speechifiers' (II. 220, 263 (c)). In the same way most theological disputes are quite absurd and the 'young fugitive' of the *Profession de foi* feels repelled by the melancholy sight of 'paradise and hell being offered as a reward for verbal games' (*PF.* 11). In the *Lettre à M. de Beaumont* Rousseau points out that most of the disputes about the origin of the world are purely verbal: few theologians, for example, understand the proper meaning of the word 'creation', the Hebrew, Greek, and Latin equivalents of which are so different from its modern meaning of 'producing something out of nothing'. Modern Christianity has become 'a certain jargon of words without ideas, with which people satisfy everything except reason' (*Œuvres* III. 73).

Unfortunately the causes of this mistaken attitude are very deeply rooted in the general corruption of human nature caused by the development of society and the corresponding distortion of natural human feelings. Men are no longer capable of heeding 'nature's gentle voice' because they have forgotten how to be themselves. As Saint-Preux well puts it in *La Nouvelle Héloïse*, 'the primary disadvantage of large towns is that men become other than what they are, and that society gives them so to speak a being different from their own' (II. 273). It will be recalled that, in Rousseau's opinion, one of the most serious symptoms of contemporary decadence is the transformation of genuine *amour de soi* into false *amour-propre*. No longer able to be himself, modern man lives 'outside himself', basing his life on 'opinion' instead of 'nature' and content to 'appear' rather than to 'be'; unlike the man who is still aware of the force of the original passion of *amour de soi*, the victim of *amour-propre* must always be comparing himself with others, thus surrendering himself to a ceaseless process of anxious reflection. The philosopher, like other men, is not animated by a genuine love of truth, but by a desire to distinguish himself from other thinkers. Pride and vanity, not a serious love of wisdom, are his constant inspirations; he seeks above all else to create a system which is his. 'Quand les philosophes seraient en état de découvrir la vérité, qui d'entre eux prendrait intérêt à elle? Chacun sait bien que son système n'est pas mieux fondé que les autres; mais il le soutient parce qu'il est à lui. . . . Où est celui qui, dans le secret de son cœur, se propose un autre objet que de se distinguer? Pourvu qu'il s'élève au-dessus du vulgaire, pourvu qu'il efface l'éclat de ses concurrents, que demande-t-il de plus? L'essentiel est de penser autrement que les autres. Chez les croyants il est athée, chez les athées il serait croyant' (*PF*. 57–59). Rousseau reverts to the same point when he insists that excessive preoccupation with intellectual knowledge will inevitably generate incredulity. Whereas it is a natural thing for the ordinary man to believe in religion, 'every learned man disdains the common sentiment; each wishes to have one that is his alone' (*PF*. 463, 471). The role of vanity in determining the contemporary philosophical outlook is a point upon which Rousseau tirelessly insists.

His dissatisfaction with contemporary philosophy does not mean that he himself is content to adopt an attitude of mere scepticism. From both the personal and the intellectual standpoint he rejects the possibility of doubt as a permanent human attitude; man has an irresistible urge to know certain truths about himself and the world, and Rousseau himself is always keenly aware of this need. Indeed, his determined, and sometimes desperate, efforts to lay down unshakable principles for his own religious life are largely inspired by an inability to remain in a state of indecision on essential issues. He tells Franquières, whose efforts to find religious truth have merely ended in 'a state of doubt': 'Je ne puis juger de cet état, parce qu'il n'a jamais été le mien. J'ai cru dans l'enfance par autorité, dans ma jeunesse par sentiment, dans mon âge mûr par raison; maintenant je crois parce que j'ai toujours cru' (*CG*. XIX. 48). Moreover, he thinks that he is not exceptional in this respect, since belief rather than doubt is the natural inclination of most men. 'Le doute sur les choses qu'il nous importe de connaître, est un état trop violent pour l'esprit humain; il n'y résiste pas longtemps; il se décide malgré lui de manière ou d'autre, et il aime mieux se tromper que ne rien croire' (*PF*. 51). It is deliberate doubt, not belief, which is unnatural to man and Rousseau professes himself incapable of understanding how anyone can be a sceptic *par système*.

The same concern with inward conviction is also apparent in Rousseau's view that the thinker's first problem is not to do away with philosophy but to understand its true function; the false psychological bias responsible for philosophical error has to be replaced by a new personal attitude capable of leading a thinker to the truth. Since most philosophers are dominated by pride and vanity, the genuine thinker must put himself in the position of sincerely *wanting* to find the truth. The Vicaire tells his young friend: 'Commencez par mettre votre conscience en état de vouloir être éclairée. Soyez sincère avec vous-même' (*PF*. 435). Sincerity is the sole basis of all sound thinking, and the Vicaire describes himself significantly as 'a man of good faith who uses his reason'. Without sincerity the search for truth will be vain; only he who earnestly wants to know the truth can ever hope to find it. In this sense a man must not begin by desiring to become a 'philosopher', in other words, by playing a role which is primarily concerned with arousing other people's admiration, but by transforming his whole philosophical endeavour into 'the love of truth'. From the very outset, therefore, the genuine thinker will realize that he can never become the uncritical disciple of another, passively taking over his opinions and accepting them as infallible truth. The priest warns his young friend of this particular danger, even as far as the exposition of his own religious beliefs is concerned. 'Appropriez-vous de mes sentiments ce qui vous aura persuadé, rejetez le reste.' 'Je vous ai déjà dit que je ne voulais pas philosopher avec vous, mais vous aider à consulter votre cœur' (id. 265). This is a natural consequence of the acceptance of sincerity as the starting-point of any fruitful philosophizing. In this respect Rousseau anticipates Kierkegaard's emphasis on the idea of personal appropriation as the necessary condition for the discovery of religious truth; remote, abstract systems can have little meaning for the living individual who seeks a philosophy that is really his. Even genuine error is far preferable to the superficial acceptance of somebody else's apparent wisdom. The Vicaire would rather have his own 'illusions' than other people's 'lies'. In any case, sincerity is likely to lead a man into truth, whereas pride and vanity never will.

Towards the end of his career Rousseau becomes increasingly inclined to treat profound personal sincerity as the distinguishing feature of his own work. In his *Lettre à M. de Beaumont* he proudly claims to have been 'sincere in everything, even against himself': unlike those hypocritical religious leaders who write for merely selfish or sectarian purposes, he has always been inspired by *la bonne foi pure et simple* and shown unswerving loyalty to his own principles. Although he has written on different subjects, he has invariably advocated 'the same morality, the same arguments, the same maxims, and, if you like, the same opinions'. Consequently it is he, and not the official representative of the Church, who is the true 'defender of God's cause' (*Œuvres*, III. 59).

To find the truth and achieve true wisdom, the man of 'good faith' must first look for it within himself; he must, as Rousseau so often puts it, *rentrer en lui-même*. This is an expression already used by Rousseau at the end of the first *Discours* and one that recurs many times in his later writings. Whatever the ultimate aim of his intellectual endeavours, the sincere thinker has to realize that the key to all valid knowledge lies 'in the nature of his own being'. No doubt he will ultimately seek to understand 'nature' in some broad, objective sense, but this extension of his knowledge can only follow, not precede, the analysis of his own being. Moreover, the foolishness of the metaphysician who, while claiming to be making an intellectual discovery, is really undertaking an illusory search for the absolute, should serve as a salutary reminder of the danger of intellectual pride. Man must begin by circumscribing the area of his investigations, and he can only do this by first of all 'withdrawing into himself' in order to find his own being. The same point is very clearly brought out in the sixth of the *Lettres morales* written for Mme d'Houdetot.

Commençons par redevenir nous, par nous concentrer en nous, par circonscrire notre âme des mêmes bornes que la nature a données à notre être; commençons en un mot par nous rassembler où nous sommes, afin qu'en cherchant à nous connaître, tout ce qui nous compose vienne à la fois se présenter à nous. Pour moi, je pense que celui qui sait le mieux en quoi consiste le moi humain est le plus près de la sagesse; et que comme le premier trait d'un dessin se forme des lignes qui le terminent, la première idée de l'homme est de le séparer de tout ce qui n'est pas lui (*CG*. III. 369–70).

Already when discussing a similar point in the fifth letter he affirms: 'De quoi s'agit-il pour cela, sinon de rentrer en soi-même, d'examiner, tout intérêt personnel à part, à quoi nos penchants naturels nous portent?' (id. 364). It is precisely because society is the source of so much error that the individual must 'withdraw into himself' in order to begin the search for truth.

As soon as the wise philosopher realizes that knowledge is first of all human and personal, he will limit his enquiries to what 'interests him immediately'—namely, the needs of his own being. Having perceived the absurdity of so many conflicting philosophical systems, the Vicaire realizes the importance of thus circumscribing the area of his enquiry. 'Le premier fruit que je tirai de ces réflexions fut d'apprendre à borner mes recherches à ce qui m'intéressait immédiatement; à me reposer dans une profonde ignorance sur tout le reste, et à ne m'inquiéter, jusqu'au doute, que des choses qu'il m'importait de savoir' (*PF.* 59). The Vicaire admirably sums up Rousseau's whole view when he affirms: 'Portant donc en moi l'amour de la vérité pour toute philosophie, et pour toute méthode une règle facile et simple, qui me dispense de la vaine subtilité des arguments, je reprends, sur cette règle, l'examen des connaissances qui m'intéressent' (*PF.* 69). In the best sense of the term the true philosopher thus learns to appreciate the value of genuine naïveté.

Rousseau's constant stress upon the restriction of knowledge to matters 'which it is important for him to know' has led a number of critics to treat him as a forerunner of 'pragmatism'.[1] Unfortunately the modern philosophical implications of this term as well as its more popular utilitarian connotation are apt to make it misleading as far as Rousseau is concerned. 'Interest', in his view, is not confined to what is practical but involves a wide range of human experience. Perhaps it would be more profitable to compare Rousseau's idea of knowledge which 'interests' us with the Kierkegaardian notion of 'interest as the rock on which metaphysics founders'. Both thinkers see 'interested knowledge' as knowledge relating directly to the needs of the living individual and requiring personal appropriation before it can acquire true validity, while this in turn involves a profound distrust of metaphysical systems which seek to swallow up the individual in some vast synthesis. The two thinkers develop the consequences of this idea of 'interest' in different ways, but their starting-point is similar enough to make the comparison suggestive.

The thinker who begins his philosophical activity with this principle of inner withdrawal is immediately vouchsafed a new source of power and inspiration. Instead of relying on nothing but a cold and sterile intellectualism, he can feel himself sustained by a genuine 'vigour of soul' which resembles the enthusiasm inspiring truly noble passions. The discovery of truth, therefore, requires 'energy of feeling' as well as intellectual acumen, and in this

---

[1] Especially P.-M. Masson and Albert Schinz. Robert Derathé, *Le Rationalisme de Rousseau* (Paris, 1948), has already emphasized the difficulty of applying the term 'pragmatism' to Rousseau's thought.

respect philosophy is animated by the impulses which lie behind other essential human activities. Lord Bomston puts the point clearly in *La Nouvelle Héloïse*: 'La sublime raison ne se soutient que par la même vigueur de l'âme qui fait les grandes passions, et l'on ne sert dignement la philosophie qu'avec le même feu qu'on sent pour une maîtresse' (II. 193). Ultimately love and wisdom come from a single source and all fundamental human qualities are imbued with the same energy. This is because both love and truth depend on the idea of perfection; they are set in motion by a 'real or chimerical object of perfection' transcending the world of sense-experience and directing the soul to the realm of the infinite. Only by withdrawing into the depths of his soul and abandoning himself to the influence of his imagination can the thinker find the origin of this 'sacred fire' and 'sacred enthusiasm' which, as Julie says, impels man towards the contemplation of the ideal possibilities of his being (II. 223).[1]

The thinker of good faith acquires a kind of intuitive perception of essential truth. 'As soon as he is willing to withdraw into himself', says Saint-Preux, 'each man feels what is good.' There is a directness and simplicity about this method which forms a striking contrast to the artificial subtlety and sophistication of contemporary philosophers. If Rousseau, as we have seen, treats subtlety as an evil, he always describes simplicity as a great good, for this is a quality rooted in the immediacy of personal experience. Having once appreciated the simplicity and directness of this approach to philosophical and religious problems, the sincere thinker is provided with a sound starting-point for all his subsequent endeavours.

However, Rousseau's frequent references to the importance of the 'inner voice' as a guide to truth does not mean that he is concerned with a merely subjective and emotional kind of philosophy. It is not a question of constructing a 'system' on the basis of some individual caprice, but of finding a valid philosophical starting-point. Like Descartes, Rousseau believes that the thinker must be provided with some primary, intuitive certainty capable of supporting all his subsequent intellectual arguments; this certainty

---

[1] Some critics have detected the influence of Plato and the Platonist tradition in this aspect of Rousseau's thought. Cf. P. Burgelin, op. cit., pp. 173 f. and C. W. Hendel, *Jean-Jacques Rousseau, Moralist* (London, 1934).

cannot be reached by mere ratiocination, but is given directly to personal consciousness. At the same time the stress upon sincerity is intended as a safeguard against any merely subjective bias. In fact, Rousseau believes that it is the grandiose metaphysical systems which are ultimately subjective, since they are not inspired by a genuine desire for truth but by their propounders' pride and vanity; as such, they are the bizarre and idiosyncratic productions of individual minds. On the other hand, the thinker of good faith will, by the very fact of penetrating to the depths of his own being, discover not only his own nature but the nature of man himself. Rather like Rousseau in the *Confessions*, and indeed Montaigne in the *Essais*, the sincere philosopher believes that an honest analysis of his own personality can serve as a *pièce de comparaison* for the whole human race. By becoming aware of his own being he will be led to the nature of man in general. If anyone sincerely asks the question 'Who am I?', he is asking it not only for himself but also for the whole human race. Rousseau, therefore, is not primarily concerned with the epistemological problem of the 'subjective' and 'objective' aspects of experience, but with its ontological foundations, in so far as these involve the need to distinguish between the artificial, accidental features of human nature and its essential, 'original' qualities. The whole object of his personal method is to enable him to escape from the pride and deceit which have bedevilled other philosophers; he wants to stand in the presence of 'nature' itself, because nature implies depth and universality. Rousseau admits that other thinkers may also recognize this point, but he believes that they have mistaken the social and historical aspects of human nature for its permanent structure. He is convinced that his method alone will allow him to penetrate to the truly original aspects of man's being, and to perceive those qualities that are 'engraved in the human heart in indelible characters'. The exploration of inner being is thus inseparable from the analysis of universal human nature.

The fact that Rousseau seeks to relate intuitively certain principles, which are revealed directly to consciousness, to the wider domain of human nature, shows that he is not prepared to dispense with reason; what he wants to do first of all is to ascertain its real function and purpose. Far from denigrating reason, he sometimes praises it so highly that certain modern commentators have not hesitated to speak of his 'rationalism'.[1] Even in a work as heavily charged with emotion as *La Nouvelle Héloïse* reason is described as 'this divine torch' which God has given men for their guidance (II. 362). Rousseau's stress upon the universality of truth also leads him to extol the benefits of reason, since 'reason is common to us all', as the Savoyard priest insists. However, it is at once apparent that the honest thinker's reason is not the 'reason' of *philosophes* who use it for the elaboration of 'subtle' arguments. Rousseau is concerned mainly with *la saine raison* or *la raison simple et primitive*, which is one of man's most 'sublime gifts'. As such it can have 'no other aim than what is good' (II. 370). Sustained by the same vigour as love itself, it enables man to distinguish permanent, universal truths from 'vain sophisms'. Through reason he can perceive the truth in 'all the clarity of primitive understanding'. 'Original' reason is frequently associated in Rousseau's mind with the image of light as well as with the idea of simplicity; it is reason that sheds light on the real nature of relationships which might otherwise be obscured by vague or confused feelings. Here again, however, it is a question of returning to a basic element of human nature, of understanding it in its authentic function, and of accepting it in all its simplicity, clarity and universality. As soon as ideas are examined *dans le silence des passions*, the most common will also be found to be the 'simplest', the most 'reasonable', and the most 'universal'. Whenever Rousseau undertakes a systematic exposition of philosophical ideas, he always emphasizes these particular characteristics. That is why he has such a great admiration for the English deist, Samuel Clarke, whose system he considers 'so striking, so luminous, so simple, and, it seems to me, offering fewer incomprehensible things to the human mind than the absurd ones that are to be found in any other system' (*PF*. 67). It is significant that in the letter to Franquières he does not hesitate to couple Clarke's name with Plato's!

One immediate cause of Rousseau's persistent refusal to abandon reason as an instrument of knowledge is its essentially 'natural' character. If all genuine human capacities are 'good', it would indeed be absurd to eliminate at the outset one of the most striking

[1] Cf., for example, Robert Derathé's *Le Rationalisme de Jean-Jacques Rousseau*, which contains a very enlightening discussion of the role of reason in Rousseau's work. Because of the considerations set out in the subsequent argument, I should not be inclined to describe Rousseau's philosophy as 'rationalist' in the traditional sense of the term.

and effective of them all. As we shall see, reason is inevitably involved in certain limitations and there may be truths which lie beyond it, but no essential truth can ever be *against* reason. The Vicaire does not hesitate to declare that 'all ideas of the deity come to us from reason alone' (*PF*. 307), whilst Julie affirms that religion can never be contrary to reason (II. 385). Moreover, one of the greatest services of reason is to protect man against the tyranny of his fellows by helping him to separate the permanent universal truths available to his own personal inspection from the predominantly irrational opinions imposed upon him by human authority. It is noteworthy, for example, that the whole of the second part of the *Profession de foi* is permeated by a strongly rationalist element, since Rousseau sees reason as a safeguard against religious intolerance and fanaticism. Modern Christianity is such a sorry and degrading spectacle, because it has become a prey to men's irrational feelings and an instrument of their pride and desire for domination. Authority all too often means force and physical constraint, whilst the 'testimony of reason itself' always makes a direct appeal to the human mind and bears witness to its own authority. Before any religious belief can be enforced it must first of all be shown to be reasonable, and once its reasonableness has been properly established, the use of force becomes either unnecessary or harmful. Man, therefore, is quite justified in opposing 'a tyranny which nature and reason disavow'.[1]

Inevitably reason must recognize its limitations as well as its powers. First of all, it may prove the existence of a reality the exact substance or essence of which it is powerless to know. Such is the case with God and the soul, realities whose existence can be rationally demonstrated but whose ultimate nature lies beyond the range of human intelligence. If in certain cases reason leads us to affirm the existence of a reality lying beyond it, it would be sheer folly to embark upon a 'metaphysical' exploration of such a mystery. In the second place, reason is only one essential element in the personality; we must not rashly assume that it can function in isolation and be the final court of appeal in all cases of doubt. Certain kinds of feeling, for example, may in some cases be more reliable guides to truth. Necessary as a means of attaining clarity

---

[1] R. Derathé (op. cit., Ch. IV, 'Les réfutations catholiques d'*Émile* au XVIIIe siècle') points out that Rousseau's Roman Catholic critics accused him of attributing excessive importance to reason.

and understanding, reason cannot provide the material for its own activity; it is incapable of supporting itself on its own foundations. Julie speaks scathingly of 'the vain sophisms of a reason which relies only on itself' (II. 359); cut off from other human powers, it will remain sterile and ineffective. It may sometimes be wise to acknowledge the importance of impulses lying beyond the range of our immediate reflection. This seems to be the point of the Vicaire's observation: 'My rule to abandon myself to feeling rather than to reason is confirmed by reason itself' (*PF*. 91). Reason, therefore, cannot provide us with the vital impulse that will enable us to act decisively in critical situations.

On the other hand, mere feeling, however powerful, simply provides the essential impulse to action; it does not give any explicit awareness of its ultimate meaning. Even the most exalted feelings must reckon with their practical effects upon the 'conduct of life', whilst in certain cases the 'heart' may be led astray by wayward passions. In other words, feelings need to be 'cultivated' in order to give us the 'truth of things', and reason must play an important part in this educative process. If feeling enables us to 'love' the good, only reason allows us to 'know' it. Cut off from the rest of man's powers, reason will undoubtedly fall into error, but as soon as it is properly related to the self's fundamental needs, its activity is certain to be beneficial.

Reason is important not simply as a means of making us aware of the truth of our being; it also enables us to discern the total pattern of our existence within the universal order. All rational truths will ultimately conform with the principle of order, whereas prejudice and arbitrary power always seek to violate it. Significantly enough, when Julie, at the time of her marriage, offers a prayer to God, she affirms: 'Je veux tout ce qui se rapporte à l'ordre de la nature que tu as établi, et aux règles de la raison que je tiens de toi' (II. 357). In the *Lettres morales* also Rousseau declares that 'la raison est la faculté d'ordonner toutes les facultés de notre âme convenablement à la nature des choses et à leurs rapports avec nous' (*CG*. III. 352). 'Par mon intelligence', declares the Vicaire, 'je suis le seul qui ait inspection sur le tout' (*PF*. 155).

In modern society erroneous views about the proper function of reason are due mainly to man's ignorance of his original nature. If in certain cases reason takes the form of a barren reflection, it can also become the tool of the artificial passions generated by civilization. In such cases it may be chasing mere 'phantoms', losing itself in an endless and futile pursuit of objectives which have little or no bearing on the problems of natural life. Society has led to a disruption and distortion of faculties, which, though good in themselves, are put to evil use. In particular, the role of reflection in modern life is a striking instance of the hypertrophy of a power that has been diverted from its proper function in the hierarchy of human values.

Yet the need to reorganize society on sound principles presupposes the co-operation of a reason restored to its real role. The rationalist vein running through the *Contrat social* is not accidental, for the establishment of civil, as opposed to natural, freedom can only be brought about through an act of will, that is, through a rational choice which sets voluntary obedience to the law and the general will above the blind impulse of appetite. True citizenship is inseparable from virtue, and virtue implies a deliberate effort which distinguishes it from merely spontaneous goodness. True morality and sociability are impossible without the help of will and reason. In Rousseau's opinion, the very fact that reason is so grievously misused in the contemporary world means that a vigorous effort must be made to restore it to its proper function; only in this way can human beings be brought together in a harmonious moral and social relationship with one another.

Rousseau believes that one of the main causes of modern man's failure to use his reason aright is his misunderstanding of the truly dynamic nature of human personality. Mankind, like the individual, has developed from a primitive and purely instinctive stage to a social mode of existence, and reason itself is a faculty that develops late, becoming effective only when man has attained moral and social consciousness. It is particularly in *Émile* that Rousseau stresses the role of reason as a power that does not function in isolation but develops in conjunction with the realization of other human potentialities.[1] From this point of view it may not be inappropriate to describe it as a 'compound' of all the rest. Educators, Rousseau points out, wrongly assume that children are rational in the adult sense. If in one way childhood is the 'sleep of reason', it also involves a limited rational activity inasmuch as reason can function in combination with the senses; children do

[1] Robert Derathé, op. cit., has stressed this developmental aspect of reason.

not use *la raison intellectuelle* but *la raison sensitive*, which operates in the domain of 'their immediate sensuous interest'. Reason, therefore, is at first individual and almost physical in its range, making use of sensations and images; only at a later stage of human development does it express a truly 'intellectual need' capable of perceiving general and abstract relationships.[1]

To be genuinely convincing, the conclusions of reason should evoke man's 'inner assent', a deeply affective response of his whole self to the truths perceived by his mind. As soon as feeling and reason are in perfect accord, it can be safely assumed that truth has at last been reached. Indeed, if truth has the rational qualities of simplicity, clarity, and universality, it must also contain a kind of 'sublimity' that owes more to the heart than the reason. Truths which 'interest' man's ultimate destiny will always have this capacity to 'lift up' his soul. It is interesting to note, for example, that Rousseau's eulogy of the philosophical system of 'the illustrious Clarke' lays special emphasis on its sublime aspect, while paying homage to the simplicity and clarity of its rational appeal; he speaks of 'this new system, so great, so consoling, so sublime, so capable of uplifting the soul, of giving a basis to virtue, and at the same time so striking, so luminous, so simple' (*PF*. 67).

To the intellectual and moral aspects of all great truths should also be added their aesthetic appeal. When, for example, in the letter to Franquières Rousseau refers to the spiritual view of the universe propounded in the works of 'a Plato' and 'a Clarke', he stresses its aesthetic value, for he speaks of 'the brilliance, simplicity, truth, and beauty of this enchanting idea' and of the appeal of 'a doctrine that is so fine, so sublime, so pleasant and so consoling for every just man' (*CG*. XIX. 51). It will be noted, therefore, that the noblest philosophy involves the luminosity and simplicity of reason, the sublimity of the heart and soul, and the beauty of aesthetic sensibility. Clarity, simplicity, sublimity, and beauty—these must be the characteristics of any philosophical system claiming our total allegiance, for truths which 'interest' us will evoke the spontaneous approval of all essential aspects of our being.

[1] R. Derathé makes a useful distinction between the psychological and metaphysical aspects of Rousseau's discussion of reason; in *Émile* he is interested primarily in its role in the development of human personality, whilst elsewhere he is concerned with its power to illuminate the structure ('order') of reality as a whole.

It is only to a limited number of fundamental truths that this criterion of complete personal response is applicable. Because of the structure of human personality, all truths will obviously not have the same degree of importance, and this is true of religious as well as of more strictly philosophical or impersonal ideas. In the *Profession de foi* Rousseau describes three categories of truth. There are, first, those truths which contain all the characteristics just enumerated, and so carry within themselves a genuine *évidence* or certainty, to which we must give our immediate assent; these are the truths to which 'in the sincerity of my heart I shall not be able to refuse my consent' (*PF*. 69). (Such, for example, is the fact of my immediate existence and my awareness of 'sensations'.) Once again, therefore, we are led back to the question of 'interest', since 'the examination of knowledge which interests me' at once eliminates any need to have recourse to 'the vain subtlety of arguments'. The second category concerns truths which have a necessary logical connexion with the first and are rationally demonstrable as deriving from them. (No doubt Rousseau would include the idea of man's 'natural goodness' and the immortality of his soul in this group.) The third kind comprises all the rest, which are thus relegated to the realm of uncertainty; we neither accept nor reject them, and do not even take the trouble to clarify them 'when they lead to nothing useful in practice'. It is perhaps to the last group alone that the popular epithet 'pragmatic' is applicable; but such truths do not embrace the whole field of human knowledge and must ultimately be related to the other two categories on which to a large extent they still depend.

These general principles are not considered by Rousseau to be merely 'philosophical' in any narrow technical sense, since he does not admit the validity of philosophy as a separate intellectual discipline. All valid forms of mental activity are inspired by the same primordial energy and ultimately converge on the same essential issues, since all are based on the indestructible unity of fundamental human experience. Instead of trying to establish a unique philosophical discipline Rousseau is concerned with an attempt to create a mental climate in which the love of truth is allowed a sincere and unrestricted expression. As we have seen, this involves a profound modification of personal attitude as well as a consequent change in intellectual habits. Since this in turn affects the whole scale of human values, philosophy and religion must ultimately be inseparable, even though at times their relationship may seem to a superficial observer remote and indirect.

2. *God and the Universe*

To understand the world the sincere thinker must first of all understand himself, for it is only through an examination of his own being that he can hope to find principles capable of guiding him in his exploration of 'nature' in a wider sense. This point of view is already apparent in Rousseau's repeated references to truths of 'immediate interest' which 'it is important for him to know'. Like most of his Locke-inspired contemporaries, he sees man as a being who is in the first instance aware of himself as a creature of 'sensations', but he refuses to limit the notion of 'interest' to the domain of sense-experience. At the outset he raises a crucial issue by asking the question: Is my 'self' to be identified with my 'sensations', or have I a distinct notion of my existence apart from these? He may well have found some helpful suggestions in Turgot's article 'Existence' in the *Encyclopédie*, which had discussed this very question.[1] Now, in Rousseau's view, the first obvious aspect of sensations is their passive nature, and this in turn means that they must originate in something outside the self; subjective sensations depend on an external object. In this way Rousseau immediately resolves—or rather eliminates—a problem upon which other philosophers like Condillac, Diderot, Turgot, and d'Alembert expended so much intellectual effort: the existence of the external world. Rousseau does not seem to have been seriously perturbed by the implications of Berkeley's idealism; he finds no difficulty in making an immediate distinction between internal and external reality, between the self and the physical world. Such a distinction, he affirms, can be readily established by a rapid analysis of sensation alone. In fact, Rousseau shows comparatively little interest in the purely objective aspects of sensation, which he takes for granted rather than proves. Admittedly, he declares that external reality may be described either in terms of isolated units ('bodies') or as a whole ('matter'), but to ask whether such bodies are real or not is, in his view, an otiose question, which can be

[1] Cf. Ronald Grimsley, 'Turgot's article "Existence" in the *Encyclopédie*', in *The French Mind: Studies in Honour of Gustave Rudler* (Oxford, 1952).

quickly abandoned for a much more interesting one: the relevance of sensation to the nature of man. More especially, he concentrates on what he considers to be an irreducible duality in the human being: if sensation is passive and ultimately determined by causes outside the self, the mind, on the other hand, is essentially active, since it does not merely submit to sensations but compares and judges them; the mind has the capacity to reach out, as it were, towards objects in order to confer meaning upon them. By this very fact it actively separates itself from the inert material supplied to it through sensations; it can compare the different qualities of sensation and consider, among other aspects, their existential status. Whereas perception is a kind of passive experience, comparison involves active judgement. It is through its power to judge sensations that the mind reveals its most characteristic function. 'Selon moi la faculté distinctive de l'être intelligent et actif est de pouvoir donner un sens à ce mot *est*' (*PF*. 81).

It is true, as M. Beaulavon points out,[1] that Rousseau here seems to accept without demur the Cartesian distinction between mind and matter as two absolutely different substances. However, he is probably more concerned with combating contemporary materialism than with developing any precise ontology of substance. In fact, while accepting Cartesian dualism in a general way, he is interested in examining the function rather than the essence of characteristic modes of being. For example, reason, as we have seen, has an important role to play in the human personality, but it combines and co-operates with other elements such as sensation and feeling. The active aspect of man's existence is not limited to his purely rational function, but forms part of his entire nature; the search for truth ultimately involves all essential elements of his being. As has already been pointed out, aesthetic and moral feeling are able to make us aware of fundamental values such as beauty, justice, and virtue. In each case we are impelled beyond our merely physical nature towards a domain of non-physical experience; our response to virtue or beauty, therefore, can be truly 'ecstatic', in the literal sense of taking us 'outside ourselves' and 'lifting us up to sublime contemplations'. It is our greatest privilege as human beings to be able to reach out in this way beyond the confines of our 'narrow soul' towards some higher realm of being.

[1] In his useful little edition of the *Profession de foi du vicaire savoyard* (Paris, 1937), p. 118, n. 1.

In *La Nouvelle Héloïse* Julie tries to explain the interdependence of personal being and objective reality. As soon as a man frees himself from the evil influence of selfish passion and reflection in order to discover the 'inner principle' or 'inner effigy' lying at the heart of his existence, he becomes conscious of an aspect of his being that is more fundamental than his sensuous or physical self. In truth, this 'effigy' acquires permanence and stability only when it is related to a perfect 'divine model', a spiritual being that is its creator; it is through the contemplation of this divine model that the human soul is purified and regenerated. Rousseau thus seems to be sympathetic to the Cartesian idea of perfection as the ground of our belief in God, but he treats this perfection as a source of enthusiasm and spiritual energy rather than a piece of rational evidence. Man's enhanced awareness of his own being and his contemplation of God as the source of all perfection are interrelated aspects of the same fundamental attitude.

Self-consciousness at the deepest level is characteristic of a being that can actively move towards the fulfilment of its own inner possibilities, and at the same time draw closer to an objective spiritual reality capable of responding to its aspirations. This means that neither man nor God must be understood in passive terms, for every sensitive being—whether it be purely spiritual like God or partly spiritual like man—is active in its essence. Even the physical aspect of human life will contain an active element that points to its spiritual origin. In short, man and the physical world are not self-explanatory but depend on the Supreme Being who created them both.

If, therefore, God's existence can be proved from the idea of perfection inherent in human nature, it can also be proved from a consideration of the external world. Rousseau probably does not attach great importance to purely philosophical arguments based on an analysis of the physical world, for he is much more interested in the examination of human nature. Nevertheless, his concern at the growing influence of materialism and atheism make him feel obliged to meet contemporary philosophers on their own ground and fight them with their own intellectual weapons. Moreover, he believes that such an approach will confirm the power of reason to adduce arguments which support the spontaneous testimony of the inner self. A long section of the *Profession de foi du vicaire savoyard* is, therefore, devoted to a reasoned proof of God's existence based on a consideration of matter in movement. To a modern reader this is the least effective part of the work, and, as Masson's edition of the *Profession de foi* shows, was probably included as an afterthought.

In Rousseau's opinion, the sight of the universe, and especially a consideration of *les choses sensibles*, should be enough to make any unbiassed observer aware of the inadequacy of materialism. The most superficial inspection of the physical world shows that matter is in a state of movement. However, since rest, not movement, is matter's natural state, movement must be imparted to it from a source outside itself. Movement may be of two kinds: 'communicated' (as when one physical object is set in motion by the impact of another) or 'spontaneous' (as when a human being wills to move a limb). Clearly, in Rousseau's view, matter is incapable of spontaneous movement, and he has no sympathy for the kind of dynamic materialism developed by Diderot. If movement is not an inherent quality of matter, it must have a non-material source, or, more precisely, a source that is in some ways analogous to its spontaneous form. In other words, the 'original' movement of matter must be related to an act of will, or to a free act that is different in quality from the necessary and determined behaviour of physical bodies. To prevent recourse to an infinite regression, we must suppose that the source of movement is ultimate and absolute, an all-powerful *will*, which may be called 'God' or the 'Supreme Being'.

A further examination of the physical universe reveals not only the presence of movement, but of matter moving in accordance with rigid laws. Characteristic of the physical world are its order and regularity—an idea that Rousseau had defended at great length in his letter to Voltaire on Providence. The universe is governed by harmony and proportion, with everything in its appointed place. As early as 1742 Rousseau had considered very sympathetically Pope's idea of a universal 'chain of beings', the whole creation being an ordered system of beings with God as their ultimate source;[1] each type of being or species is distinct and rigidly separated from the rest, the absence of intermediate links revealing the fixity of the universal order. Rousseau never showed any sympathy for Diderot's view of the universe as matter in a state of continuous transformation or evolution; ultimately

[1] *Corresp. complète*, I. 132–43. Cf., *supra*, p. 18.

the universe must be considered as a unity with each category of being having its own place and function within the whole. Even though I cannot perceive the universe as a whole and must admit that everything is moving towards 'an end which it is impossible for me to perceive', the sight of the 'harmony of beings and the admirable concurrence of each part for the preservation of the whole' enables me to obtain at least some insight into the meaning of the great design governing the physical structure of the world. Every unprejudiced observer, believes Rousseau, must acknowledge 'the unity of intention which is revealed in the relations of all the parts of this great whole' (*PF*. 137). In this way the Supreme Being is shown to be not merely absolute will but also absolute *intelligence*.

Rousseau believes that a further consideration of the universe will reveal not only the power and intelligence but also the goodness of its Creator. In his view, this is an inevitable consequence of God's omnipotence. Furthermore, Rousseau refuses to admit that the alleged presence of 'physical evil' can seriously impugn the idea of divine goodness. Already in his long letter to Voltaire in 1756 he tries to deal with this problem, and in 1769 he returns to it more briefly in his correspondence with Franquières. To Voltaire he points out that it is very easy and misleading for man to judge the whole universe from his own very restricted viewpoint. For example, the alleged 'irregularity', through which Crousaz had tried to refute Pope's optimism, may simply be due to ignorance of natural laws: nature always acts in obedience to the law of cause and effect, but to a limited human understanding the connexion may not be obvious. Voltaire's assertion that nature does not act rigorously is merely an unproved assumption based on abstract mathematical principles which may not have any direct bearing upon the structure of the physical universe: to make confident assertions about the ultimate nature of the universe we should have to understand it in all its complexity; mathematical rules based on the observation of a few isolated 'natural bodies' cannot be accepted as a final explanation of the meaning of physical reality as a whole. An even greater error is for man to consider the universe in the light of his own selfish needs; and following the popular views associated with Pope and Leibniz, Rousseau points out that a 'particular evil' may turn out to be a 'good' when seen in relation to the universe as a complete system of being. Sometimes the sacrifice of an individual's happiness may be necessary for the preservation of the whole. Even death, which from the point of view of most men seems an undoubted evil, may simply be part of the entire natural process, a means of securing the continuation of the species through the fertilization of the earth! If we take a still wider view of the problem, it is surely absurd of human pride to suppose that this little world of ours is the only one that counts in God's eyes and that He has created the whole vast universe for the sake of a tiny part rather than for the good of the whole!

In any case, it is man rather than nature that is responsible for the problem of 'physical evil'. The disastrous consequences of the Lisbon earthquake, which Voltaire finds an unmitigated evil, were largely due to human folly, and especially to men's obstinate determination to live huddled together in cities instead of leading the isolated, scattered existence prescribed for them by nature. In the *Discours sur l'inégalité* Rousseau tries to develop the same point by showing that man's anxious concern with sickness and death is the product of his civilized environment; many evils of modern life were unknown to primitive man, who accepted death and illness as part of the natural process of life. Man has brought into existence much evil and unhappiness by his misuse of natural resources and the desperate pursuit of mistaken goals. The alleged existence of physical evil is thus no valid argument against the goodness of the universe.

Less intellectual but equally convincing evidence of the divine origin of the universe is to be found in its astonishing beauty. Rousseau himself, of course, has a particularly strong 'feeling for nature', which, as we have seen, is frequently imbued with religious significance, but he also believes that beauty is an essential feature of the physical world, accessible to all men prepared to open their eyes to its enchanting appeal. It will be recalled that the Vicaire himself begins his profession of faith by taking his young protégé to the top of a hill dominating the river Po, from which they can contemplate the sunlit plains and the 'vast chain of the Alps'. 'On eût dit que la nature étalait à nos yeux toute sa magnificence pour en offrir le texte à nos entretiens' (*PF*. 35). The 'order of the world' thus appeals not only to man's intellect, but also to an aesthetic sensibility that is capable of leading him to 'sublime contemplations'. In this way the religious interpretation of the universe is in perfect harmony with the personal attitude involved in any serious pursuit of fundamental truth: aesthetic as well as intellectual and moral factors induce man to acknowledge the beauty, power, order, and goodness of God's handiwork.

The universe, therefore, reveals God's existence in a number of ways, each basic aspect of man's personality responding to the mystery of the divine Creation. If intellectual knowledge is necessarily incomplete, there are other elements in man's nature which provide him with surer insight into the meaning of physical nature, through an ecstatic, expansive identification of his inner self with the universal system of which it forms part. This is an experience which Rousseau has described with great lyrical power in various parts of his personal writings, but it is also one which must ultimately accord with the conclusions drawn from a more detached and rational examination of the world. All aspects of man's being thus finally lead him to acknowledge God as the source not only of his own being but also of the whole universal system to which he belongs.

3. *Man's Inner Life*

Although Rousseau's discussion of the problem of God's existence reveals his reluctance to lay undue stress upon purely metaphysical arguments, his growing concern with the influence of materialism impelled him, as we have seen, to make some concession to contemporary philosophical habits, and explains many of the later modifications and additions to the *Profession de foi*. More especially the publication of Helvétius's *De l'Esprit* in 1758 made the refutation of philosophical materialism seem particularly urgent. However, the long letter to Voltaire on Providence already shows that he was not always happy or effective in metaphysical discussion, for it concludes with an explosive outburst of feeling which subordinates intellectual difficulties to the evidence of inner feeling and personal conviction. Whatever may be the philosophical objections to religious principles, Rousseau affirms his own profound need to believe in them.[1] His refusal to allow 'all the subtleties of metaphysics' to affect his personal faith in the immortality of the soul and the beneficence of Providence is typical of his attitude towards most religious issues. Having once proved the bare

---

[1] Cf., *supra*, p. 18.

fact of God's existence, he limits an examination of His being to those aspects which have some bearing on human needs. 'Pénétré de mon insuffisance,' says the Savoyard priest, 'je ne raisonnerai jamais sur la nature de Dieu, que je n'y suis forcé par le sentiment de ses rapports avec moi' (*PF*. 153). If it is impossible to contemplate God himself, our own need will reveal those aspects of His being which are of 'immediate interest' to us. Intelligence, power, goodness, and beauty we can rationally apprehend as necessary constituents of the divine being, but they become genuinely significant only when they are related to the demands of our inner life.

As soon as he is conscious of the majesty of God's being, man, insists Rousseau, can see his own existence in a proper perspective and realize the absurdity of petty egoism. Henceforth he is provided with a firm foundation not only for his relationship with the outside world but also for the fulfilment of his own possibilities. The wise man will acquiesce in the order of the world and not try to change it for his own purposes; he will make himself the instrument of God's purpose instead of pursuing the gratification of his own selfish desires. (The wicked man, on the other hand, seeks obstinately to subordinate the world to his own needs and so violates the principle of order lying at the heart of the universal creation.) An awareness of God's existence allows a man to attain a more balanced view of his own being, for as well as being drawn to God by his contemplation of the divine order, he is aware of an imperative need to distinguish between the essential and the inessential elements in his own personality.

It is, therefore, not surprising to find Rousseau resuming, after his long discussion of God and the physical universe, his earlier analysis of man's inner life, for it is towards a discussion of this issue that the whole argument is implicitly directed. If the duality of human nature, as already revealed in the contrast between the passivity of sensation and the activity of judgement, causes man to interpret the world in the light of its spiritual origin, further reflection on his own inner life can lead to a consciousness of God's being by another and more direct route. More especially, man's active nature is expressed not only through his intellect, but also through the power of his will to choose between good and evil. In short, it is not only his active judgement but also—and especially— his freedom of will which offers further evidence of his religious destiny. The *Discours sur l'inégalité* had shown man to be endowed with the possibility of freedom even at the most rudimentary state of his existence, even though it only became active at a later and more complex stage of development. In subsequent works Rousseau was to treat freedom as the most fundamental and characteristic feature of human nature, the ultimate quality distinguishing man from the beast. Just as he can choose between the passivity of sensation and the activity of judgement, so can man become the slave of bodily passions or, by an effort of will and free choice, pursue some higher principle like virtue. Furthermore, Rousseau believes that the freedom of the will eventually serves as a proof of the immortality of the soul. Since freedom is revealed by our ability to resist the tyranny of bodily needs, the quality enabling us to do this must be non-physical or immaterial; freedom involves the reality of a unique, indestructible substance which must continue to exist after the dissolution of the body to which it is attached. Already in this life our awareness of freedom should help us to acknowledge the existence of a spiritual element that cannot be identified with physical or bodily appetites: this is the 'divine model' or 'simulacrum', the 'inner effigy', which, as we have seen, every God-created human being carries within him.[1] Whether he is conscious of it or not, a free being's greatest privilege is to strive for the fulfilment of this divine ideal.

If the true value of freedom is made manifest through man's choice of a noble ideal, modern life offers sad evidence of his frequent misuse of this God-given power. Freedom, like reason, can be applied to unworthy ends that run counter to the ordered beauty of the universal system. 'Le tableau de la Nature ne m'offrait qu'harmonie et proportions, celui du genre humain ne m'offrait que confusion, désordre! Le concert règne entre les éléments et les hommes sont dans le chaos!' (*PF.* 167.) This contradiction is due to the radical dualism of human nature already described: if man is often drawn towards 'the study of eternal truths', love of justice and *le beau moral*, as well as towards the 'regions of the intellectual world the contemplation of which is the sage's delight', he can also become the slave of his senses and passions, the prisoner of selfish desires that shut him off from all that should extend and exalt his being. He is, therefore, both free and enslaved—free when he heeds reason and wills the good, enslaved when he is dominated by base passions.

[1] Cf., *supra*, p. 54.

Perhaps freedom's noblest achievement is to enable man to follow the promptings of his most fundamental attribute, namely, the primordial feeling of 'conscience'. Conscience is the surest guide of 'an ignorant and limited being' who is also 'intelligent and free'. Conscience is the vital impulse which makes freedom morally significant, for it is the 'infallible judge of good and evil'. In a justly famous passage of the *Profession de foi* Rousseau has paid eloquent homage to this 'divine instinct', to this 'immortal, celestial voice', which makes us worthy of our Creator. Conscience is the divine spark within us—not some rare, freakish quality (even though it may seem so to men corrupted by the insidious influence of 'civilization'), but the very essence of our nature as moral beings. If it lifts us up to God, conscience is also the 'sacred voice of nature', the spontaneous impulse which makes us aware of our fundamental humanity. This is our most 'original' feature, for it is the 'voice of the soul', just as the passions are 'the voice of the body'. When every other human capacity seems impotent, when reason is involved in doubt and uncertainty or the heart beset by unruly passions, conscience will never fail to succour those who listen to a voice that speaks 'the sweetest, purest, and most energetic language of virtue' (I. 687). At such times man's wisest course is to heed this inner voice *dans le silence des passions*, for it will protect him against the promptings of his own selfish nature, 'the errors of reason', and the insidious influence of worldly 'maxims'.

To those who desire an objective proof of the truth of conscience —and, in particular, Rousseau is thinking of those contemporaries who have been led astray by a materialistic philosophy that dismisses conscience and remorse as mere 'prejudices or chimeras', and treats vice and virtue as the merely artificial products of environment, with no autonomous value—there is available the evidence of human nature: the 'manifest, universal agreement of every nation' and the 'remarkable uniformity of men's judgement' show that all people possess the same basic sense of right and wrong. What is more dishonest or futile, therefore, than Montaigne's pathetic efforts to unearth 'in some corner of the world a custom opposed to notions of justice'? How can some rare exception count against 'this principle admitted and recognized by the whole human race'? An impartial analysis of human habits shows that behind the prodigious variety of judgements and opinions there persist 'the same ideas of justice and honesty'. Objective observation thus confirms inner conviction. In any case, the sincere seeker of truth will not need to look so far, for, observing its power in his own life, he will find that 'the voice of conscience speaks for itself'.

That the power of conscience should be immediately evident to the inner self is not unexpected when we remember that, in Rousseau's view, conscience is a feeling rather than a judgement, and, as such, has the directness and simplicity of 'nature' itself. Man does not need, says Rousseau, the 'frightening apparatus of philosophy' or 'the subtleties of reasoning' to prove the reality of a fundamental feeling which every sincere human being can experience for himself. Moreover, to the simplicity of its appeal must also be added the 'sublimity' of *cette sainte et bienfaisante voix* which evokes a heart-felt response in every man ready to make use of nature's most precious gift.

Although the unique role of conscience becomes particularly striking in moments of great personal crisis, when men are in desperate need of special help and guidance, it would be wrong to isolate it from other natural powers. Its apparently exceptional quality is largely due to the corruption of a society that has alienated man from his true self. It is contemporary decadence which makes it necessary for conscience to protect people against the vagaries of reason and passion; in themselves reason and passion are not bad, but only become so when they are allowed to disrupt the harmonious balance of natural qualities by claiming supreme authority. In this way they are made, as has been shown, the instruments of pride and self-interest, in a word, of that *amour-propre* which has everywhere usurped the authority of authentic *amour de soi*. In a regenerated society, on the other hand, conscience would be as natural and spontaneous as any other natural gift, co-operating with reason and freedom to secure the perfect fulfilment of the human being.

Because conscience is rooted in a feeling or 'instinct' which moves us to 'love' the good, it does not follow that it has any specific *knowledge* of the good. Although this innate feeling spontaneously impels us towards the good, 'independently of reason', it still needs to be developed. If we never become aware of conscience through the sole activity of a reason which, as we have seen, cannot be sustained by its own resources and is powerless without the inspiration of feeling, reason does at least help us to perceive and understand more clearly the object of our fundamental feeling; through it we can know that a particular object is worthy of our affection, and as soon as we become aware of this, conscience will impel us to love it.[1] 'Sitôt que sa raison le lui fait connaître, sa conscience la porte à l'aimer; c'est ce sentiment qui est inné' (*PF*. 269). Conscience provides the original impetus, the primordial urge, which makes possible man's awareness and pursuit of goodness. Clearly, however, it is the whole of man's being, not some particular part of it, that is involved in the fulfilment of his moral obligations.

Such an attitude will expose the error of any moral outlook based on a narrow conception of self-interest. This does not mean that Rousseau believes in the possibility of a purely disinterested morality, for he constantly insists that man will always act 'for his own good'. As he tells d'Offreville, to expect man to obey any other motive is quite chimerical and contrary to the demands of his inmost nature; it is absurd to suppose that he will be easily persuaded to sacrifice everything to the public good, since his actions must always bear some relationship to his own needs.[2] The materialists' error, therefore, is not to have rejected impersonal morality, but to have defined 'interest' in an excessively egoistic sense. *Amour de soi*, true 'self-love', is an 'original' absolute passion, which is the source of all the rest; without it man could never be a real self. *Amour-propre*, on the other hand, is a relative, artificial state of mind produced by the social environment, one that makes a man compare himself with others and base his life on 'opinion' instead of on the promptings of 'nature'. Whereas *amour de soi* spontaneously seeks the good and finds a deep satisfaction in doing it, *amour-propre* is involved in a perpetual reflection, which anxiously relates everything to the individual's own selfish desires. Consequently, whilst *amour de soi* is a naturally expansive impulse, 'a state of strength which extends us beyond ourselves', as Rousseau puts it in *Émile*, *amour-propre* merely contracts personal existence by inducing a man to live outside himself and sacrifice 'reality' and 'being' to the illusions of mere 'appearance' and 'opinion'. The former leads naturally to fulfilment in the love of our fellow men and a harmonious relationship with the order of the

---

[1] Cf., *supra*, pp. 47–8.
[2] Cf. the important letter of 4 October 1761 (*CG*. VI. 222–8).

physical universe; the latter finds happiness only in the misfortune and humiliation of other people.

Evil, therefore, is not a genuinely integral part of human nature, one of its original features. Man is naturally good, not wicked. No sane man, insists Rousseau, will do evil for its own sake, and the notion of 'original sin' is dismissed as quite untenable. The wicked man is the one whose natural goodness has been stifled by pride, passion, and selfish reflection; he is the unfortunate victim of a society which makes it very difficult for people to know and follow the inclination of their natural feelings; everything leads to the triumph of narrow selfish interests which prevent men from being completely themselves. This means that evil is less primordial than good. 'Moral evil' (for we have seen that, in Rousseau's opinion, 'physical evil' does not constitute a serious problem) is derived from man's misuse of his freedom: he weakly abandons himself to the physical aspects of his being (bodily appetites and passions), or else allows his reason to become corrupted by pernicious social influences that contract and distort his personality instead of encouraging the development of its natural potentialities. Evil comes from an abandonment to the passive elements in our being, whereas goodness presupposes a willingness to follow actively the impulses of nature. No doubt in modern society the spontaneity of good feelings has almost completely vanished; to recover true goodness would require a heroic effort of will, the deliberate affirmation of a 'virtue' which can resist the insidious temptations of social values. But as soon as we succeed in identifying ourselves with the force or power of virtue, we find 'deep satisfaction in triumphing over our passions and reigning over our hearts'. 'Force invincible de la vertu, nul ne te connaît que celui qui sent tout son être, et qui sait qu'il n'est pas au pouvoir des hommes d'en disposer!' (*CG*. XIX. 59). Virtue is the greatest proof of our freedom and so of our ability to rise above the demands of 'necessity' by an effort of will. Through virtue we are brought to the true fulfilment of our destiny as moral and spiritual beings.

A problem like that of evil, which seems very perplexing to the 'subtle' minds of philosophers and theologians, ceases to be a source of anxious reflection as soon as it is related to authentic human experience. Rousseau is never tired of insisting that the 'subtlety' of many philosophical problems is not capable of withstanding the 'simplicity' and 'sublimity' of genuine personal feelings. In any case, as we have already seen from his examination of the various questions raised by man's position in the world, the conclusions of reason have to be confirmed by the testimony of inner assent: we must be inwardly convinced of the truth of our intellectual principles, and this is possible only when our reasons are subjected to the free and spontaneous response of deeper feelings. Although such a test often serves to confirm the validity of our philosophical ideas, it may also expose the fallacies of superficial or dishonest reasoning, because the reaction of the whole self is more trustworthy than the evidence of a single part. 'Existence' as a whole may suggest a truth that eludes the activity of reason alone, and it is to the primordial testimony of existence itself that Rousseau constantly returns.

It is noteworthy that although the letter on Providence attempts to refute by means of reasoned arguments Voltaire's objections to the goodness of God's creation, it lays even greater stress on the notion of existence. Whatever may be the theoretical conclusions drawn by pessimists from the pain, cruelty, and injustice of human life, Rousseau points out that most men find in the mere fact of their existence a satisfaction that outweighs the effect of all their sufferings and misfortunes. In spite of the most adverse circumstances, existence is felt to be valuable in its own right. Whereas Providence has arranged for the position of every 'material being' to be determined by its relation to the whole physical system, in the moral sphere the value of 'every intelligent and sensitive being' is grounded in its own existence. Since man is a moral and spiritual agent, the ultimate meaning of his being does not depend on his body or physical environment, but upon the free acceptance of a personal and intrinsically valuable existence. Furthermore, as has already been pointed out, freedom presupposes the presence of a spiritual element in man, so that the mere enumeration of physical evils, however many or dreadful, can never impugn the spiritual and moral basis of his being. It is better for man to exist than not to exist, whatever the particular evils and limitations of his material condition; to exist 'according to his own nature' is his greatest privilege, and this supreme fact overshadows all the rest. Moreover, Rousseau points out that the value of existence must be judged in terms of its total duration and not of one small portion; since man's freedom postulates his immortality, due consideration must be given to the prolongation of his existence in the next world. But even in this earthly sphere it is already clear to the man who knows how to appreciate it that 'the sweet enjoyment of life is permanent' (*CG*. XIX. 56). 'Supreme enjoyment', affirms the Vicaire, 'is in contentment with oneself' (*PF*. 191). The proper goal of human life is, therefore, happiness, that is, the enjoyment of existence: to exist is to be oneself in absolute plenitude, 'without division or obstacle'. This is the simplest and yet richest possibility of our entire being, the one that gives us a true foretaste of the perfect bliss that awaits the good man in the life to come.

That the source of all true happiness lies within ourselves is apparent at even the most rudimentary stage of existence, and becomes still more evident as man develops the 'original' possibilities of his nature. Primitive man, as Rousseau points out in the *Discours sur l'inégalité*, already enjoys 'the feeling of his existence', although it is largely an instinctive feeling associated with the need for self-preservation. But this is precisely what civilized people have forgotten—that primitive man's happiness is derived mainly from his effortless acceptance of the immediate consciousness of his existence. No doubt such a mode of being would not be appropriate for a more highly developed personality, but the essential principle remains true—that 'natural' man can find happiness in the enjoyment of his own being, whatever its particular stage of development. In his last years Rousseau himself, through the experience of reverie, was to enjoy the 'feeling of his existence' in its most highly developed form, and to become aware that 'the feeling of existence devoid of any other affection is by itself a precious feeling of contentment and peace'. At such times he enjoyed 'a full, perfect, and sufficient happiness'. Ultimately an experience such as this could only strengthen his belief in immortality, for it seemed to hold out the hope of a still higher form of 'felicity'.

Rousseau's excessive emphasis upon the subjective aspect of this experience in his last years was probably due to acute inner tension, and, in particular, to his awareness of himself as an innocent man persecuted by a hostile society. In his less exalted moments, he acknowledged that the feeling of existence did not restrict but rather extended the self; while enhancing the sense of personal reality, it also initiated a movement outwards towards the objective world. Authentic *amour de soi* is, therefore, expansive as well as intensive. More especially, it is inseparable from the 'order' governing the whole universe, and man's existence as a self involves his participation in the universal system of which it forms part. Both man and the physical world are God's creation and provide unmistakable evidence of their spiritual origin. As he becomes conscious of his true nature, man perceives the profound *convenance* existing between his immortal soul and the spiritual principle embodied in the physical order of the universe.

At a lower psychological level man's expansive impulses already bring him into contact with the world of nature, and in the *Confessions* Rousseau speaks very eloquently of the period of life when 'its expansive plenitude extends, so to speak, our being through all our sensations and embellishes for us the whole of nature with the charm of our existence' (I. 58). At certain privileged moments the self can become ecstatically identified with the 'universal order'. 'Je sens des extases, des ravissements inexprimables à me fondre pour ainsi dire dans le système des êtres, à m'identifier avec la nature entière' (I. 1065–6). Even when these intense feelings are lacking, Rousseau believes that man can always find satisfaction in the contemplation of an order that harmonizes with the ultimate possibilities of his own being and reveals the meaning of his spiritual destiny. Already in his feeling for nature he can become confident of his immortality. 'J'acquiesce', says the Vicaire, 'à l'ordre qu'il [Dieu] établit, sûr de jouir moi-même un jour de cet ordre et d'y trouver ma félicité; car quelle félicité plus douce que de se sentir ordonné dans un système où tout est bien?' (*PF.* 285). In this unmistakable anticipation of our immortality we can look forward to the time when, 'delivered from the illusions of our body and senses, we shall enjoy the contemplation of the Supreme Being'.

Such an attitude is not concerned primarily with understanding the universe but with entering into communion with its Creator. 'Je médite sur l'ordre de l'univers, non pour l'expliquer par de vains systèmes, mais pour l'admirer sans cesse, pour adorer le sage Auteur qui s'y fait sentir. Je converse avec lui, je pénètre toutes mes facultés de sa divine essence' (*PF.* 293). Through the contemplation of the universe, therefore, the self is lifted up to its Creator. 'C'est m'élever à ma source que de te méditer sans cesse.' To be overwhelmed by God's majesty and even to feel 'annihilated' in his presence is the supreme way of achieving personal fulfilment.

This way of looking at the universe involves a predominantly contemplative attitude. The self is identified with the sense of its own existence as an absolute good in so far as it does not seek to ask for anything further than this experience of supreme felicity in God's presence. Man does not need to pray in any conventional sense, for his sole prayer is 'Thy will be done'! 'Je m'attendris à ces bienfaits, je le bénis de ses dons; mais je ne le prie pas' (*PF*. 293). This suggests a mood of adoration and admiration rather than an active petitioning for specific favours; in adoration man goes beyond any mere asking, for he anticipates, as it were, the fulfilment that awaits him in the next world. 'C'est pour m'élever d'avance autant qu'il se peut à cet état de bonheur, de force et de liberté que je m'exerce aux sublimes contemplations.' Moreover, it is precisely through 'this state of happiness, strength and freedom' that the personality can achieve an exalted sense of unity and harmony. The contemplation of the 'divine model' will also 'purify' and 'lift up' the soul, as Julie affirms, and so make it aware of those 'sublime truths' which constitute the ultimate goal and value of its existence. Through contemplation the self is brought into harmony with God and the universal order he has created.

No doubt contemplation has its dangers, as Saint-Preux points out, for over-indulgence can lead to a passive attitude that ignores moral and social responsibilities; all too often the mystic's ecstasy makes him indifferent to the practical tasks of life and isolates him from his fellows. Even Rousseau himself was aware of his own dangerous predilection for this passive kind of contemplation, and in his last work described himself as 'dévot à la manière de Fénelon'. Generally speaking, however, he believes that the 'charms of contemplation' are intended to strengthen, not weaken, our humanity and encourage us in the active performance of our duties by making us aware of the ultimate spiritual significance of all finite activities.

4. *Natural Religion and Revealed Religion*

The main purpose of Rousseau's frequent references to the existential basis of religious values is to evoke his reader's active response to his own spiritual possibilities; ultimately all talk about religion must be directed towards an awakening of religious experience itself. To achieve this end Rousseau is first of all concerned with removing obstacles which stand in the way of spiritual fulfilment; he wants to enable the individual to establish direct contact with the source of religious truth. That is why he lays so much stress on the simplicity of principles which, being immediately related to the needs of the individual himself, have nothing in common with the subtleties of abstract reasoning. Moreover, Rousseau's belief in natural goodness strengthens his confidence in man's ability to save himself by his own efforts: God has given him the power to find the truth which 'interests' his personal existence. This is, in fact, the fundamental point at issue between Rousseau and his contemporaries: he decisively rejects the idea of a Church claiming a unique revelation, for, in his view, this falsely presupposes that members of a particular ecclesiastical organization have a way of finding the truth that is denied to other people. Rousseau, on the other hand, believes that God has effectively revealed himself through the 'eyes', 'conscience', and 'judgement' of the individual who is prepared to seek him in sincerity and good faith; God has shown himself to men through 'his works' and 'their hearts'. To find God man has only to make 'good use of his faculties'. The authority of other men, with their claim to privileged knowledge, is a serious hindrance to the experience of genuine religion, which every man must and can discover for himself in the simplicity of his own heart and 'in the silence of the passions'. 'How many men between God and me!' cries the Vicaire as he calls attention to one of the most persistent evils of orthodox religion.[1]

To the objection that the individual is incapable of finding the truth for himself because of his limited natural powers, Rousseau replies that this is an aspect of the human condition from which nobody is exempt. Moreover, the sincere individual who wisely confines himself to the pursuit of truths which 'it is important for him to know' is far more favourably placed than organized groups of men corrupted by pride and vanity. 'Si j'exerce ma raison, si je la cultive, si j'use bien des facultés immédiates que Dieu me donne, j'apprendrais de moi-même à le connaître, à l'aimer, à aimer ses œuvres, à vouloir le bien qu'il veut, et à remplir pour lui plaire tous mes devoirs sur la terre. Qu'est-ce que tout le savoir des

---

[1] Rousseau's attitude towards Christianity is discussed by R. Derathé in an article, 'Jean-Jacques Rousseau et le Christianisme', in the *Revue de Métaphysique et de Morale*, LIII (1948), pp. 378–414.

hommes m'apprendra de plus?' (*PF*. 397). The reasoning of other men, dominated and perverted by *amour-propre*, can add nothing to the sincere use of my own mind and will almost certainly lead me astray. 'Tout ce qu'un homme connaît naturellement, je puis aussi le connaître, et un autre homme peut se tromper aussi bien que moi.' Ultimately, therefore, a man cannot avoid the responsibility of having to judge for himself! The test of religious truth does not consist of conformity with the opinion of others, but of the 'clear, sublime and striking' evidence of principles based on conscience and reason. Nothing, therefore, could be more foolish than to allow the 'authority of God speaking to my reason' to be supplanted by the errors and caprices of human authority.

Rousseau's animadversions against human authority are strengthened by his conviction that religious ideas, like all others, have been corrupted by the influence of society, which incites men to intolerance and fanaticism. The claim to possess exclusive religious truth is usually accompanied by a desire to satisfy the most selfish and ferocious passions. In this respect Rousseau's criticism of established religion is not very different from that of the *philosophes*, although he does relate it more closely to his view of society as a whole. Theologians, like philosophers, are particularly susceptible to the influence of pride and vanity, and seek constantly to dominate other people's minds. Religious intolerance is worse than other kinds, because it is found in men whose lives are supposed to be devoted to the service of Christian love.

Of the various forms of human authority the most insidious, in Rousseau's view, is the one which relies on books. Authentic religious education, like all education, can never be effectively based on books, for these merely perpetuate the errors of *amour-propre*. To look for truth in the printed word is to become lost in the myriad of competing views and systems by which men try to impose their will on other people. Books, like other forms of authority, are the product of a corrupt social environment and, in a still more general sense, reflect all the limitations of the social and historical process: pride, envy, love of power, these and other vices are characteristic of a society which has sacrificed *amour de soi* to the claims of *amour-propre*. Reliance on bookish authority is a sign that man has once again abandoned the lessons of 'nature' for the illusions of 'opinion'. It is thus not surprising that the Vicaire should declare that he has 'closed all books in order to open the book of nature'. This is indeed, in Rousseau's opinion, the only authority in which man can place absolute trust and the only means through which he can hope to recover the simplicity of authentic religious experience.

This profound distrust of authority and the consequent eulogy of man's natural powers as an instrument for the discovery of religious truth explains the strongly 'rationalist' character of the second part of the *Profession de foi*, which some critics have deemed to be inconsistent with the 'sentimental' basis of the first part. However, it has already been pointed out that to establish an absolute antithesis between feeling and reason is to misunderstand an outlook which seeks to do justice to both. To be sure, the needs of a particular argument may cause Rousseau to give prominence to some particular aspect of human nature. Since, for example, religious authority has been corrupted by irrational social influences, it should be restored to its proper place and function by the wise exercise of reason, which unerringly reveals the clarity and simplicity of original truth. On other occasions, however, natural feeling may be invoked to restrain and correct the ambitious claims of a reasoning divorced from those very powers by which it should be constantly sustained.

Rousseau's condemnation of bookish authority in religious matters does not include the Gospels, which, he affirms, have the unique merit of expressing the principal qualities of natural religion; they contain a 'simplicity' that wins the immediate approval of reason and a 'sublimity' that appeals directly to the heart. Nothing can equal the 'majesty' and 'holiness' of a book whose dogmas are so simple and morality so sublime. The constant application of the two epithets, 'simple' and 'sublime', to the Gospels suggests that the biblical message is in perfect harmony with the conclusions of reason and nature. But this means also that the Gospels must not be treated primarily as historical evidence; 'this sacred book' is remarkable for the rationality and sublimity of its teaching rather than for the uniqueness of the events it describes. Its undoubted historical veracity is not guaranteed by the approbation of any external authority, but by its ability to satisfy our reason and conscience; the immediate, spontaneous assent of our inner being to the Gospel message is enough to convince us that it cannot have been invented by human imagination. In other words, the validity of the Gospel is not based on historical 'facts' and 'evidence' but on the irrefragable testimony of human nature itself. Undoubtedly historical considerations may help to strengthen our inner conviction. For example, an examination of the outlook of Jesus's Jewish contemporaries clearly shows that they could never have discovered by their own efforts principles which were beyond their comprehension. History, however, merely supports the conclusions of nature; it can never be authoritative in its own right or run counter to the lessons of nature. Ultimately it is reason and conscience, not history, that provide us with adequate criteria for distinguishing between truth and falsehood. Our understanding of any religious text involves 'a submission to the authority of God and reason, which must precede that of the Bible, and which serves as its foundation' (*CG.* VI. 96). It must be admitted, insists Rousseau, that in spite of its astonishing sublimity, 'this same Gospel is full of incredible things, of things which are repugnant to reason, and which it is impossible for any sensible man to conceive or to admit' (*PF.* 413–14). Inevitably, therefore, it is man's natural powers and 'the unalterable order of nature', not some arbitrary authority, which must determine his final attitude towards the 'sacred book'.

However, the compelling force of the Gospels does not rest solely on their 'elevated pure morality'. The striking personality of Jesus himself—a unique example of a man living out the truths he so fearlessly teaches—gives them powerful and convincing support. Particularly remarkable is the contrast between Jesus as the embodiment of 'the simplicity of the most heroic virtues' and the Jews as an example of 'the basest nation' of their day. The greatness of Jesus becomes especially obvious when he is compared with one of the most respected philosophers of antiquity, Socrates. The latter undoubtedly died like a sage, nobly and courageously, but without great pain and supported until the very end by the admiration and affection of his friends; even as a philosopher he invented nothing, since he drew on the wisdom of his predecessors; had it not been for his honourable death, says Rousseau, Socrates would probably have been known to posterity as a mere sophist. If the Greek philosopher drew strength and knowledge from his environment, Jesus had no such force to help him: he was alone in a hostile environment. 'From the heart of the most furious fanaticism the highest wisdom made itself heard.' Still more horrible and heart-rending was the manner of his death as a criminal expiring in torment, 'insulted, mocked at, cursed by a whole nation', and yet praying to God for the salvation of those who are putting him to death. 'Socrates taking the poisoned cup blesses the man who offers it to him with tears; Jesus, in the midst of frightful torment, prays for his merciless executioners' (*PF.* 411). In a famous sentence Rousseau sums up the essential difference between the two: 'Yes, if the life and death of Socrates are those of a sage, the life and death of Jesus are those of a God.' But this comparison is meant to show the superiority of Jesus; it does not imply an acceptance of his divinity. For Rousseau Jesus was no doubt unique, but as a 'divine man', not as the Son of God. He was not the God-Man of orthodox Christian tradition, but a perfect example of nature's noblest qualities.

At times Rousseau can wax eloquent, even sentimental, over the figure of Jesus: in the third of the *Lettres écrites de la Montagne* he describes Jesus's morality as having 'something attractive, seductive and tender' and his character as being that of 'a man of good society' with a 'sensitive heart'. 'If he had not been the wisest of mortals, he would have been the most likable' (III. 754). That Rousseau considered Jesus as the founder of natural religion and the remarkable embodiment of its human qualities is also revealed by a curious tendency in his later years to see himself as a Christ-like figure, for was not Jean-Jacques also—though to a lesser degree perhaps—a remarkable example of the simple, good man persecuted by a wicked world?[1]

Our acknowledgement of Jesus's authority is thus due to the way in which he exemplifies the authentic qualities of the natural man, qualities which make an immediate appeal to our conscience and reason. According to Rousseau, the error of Jesus's contemporaries and successors was to have forgotten this simple but vital fact. Already the principles of 'natural religion' as advocated by Jesus were corrupted by St. Paul and later by the Church. In at least one place Rousseau stresses that Jesus's first intention was to 'raise up' his own nation and make it a 'free people' (*CG.* XIX. 62). As the eighteenth-century *philosophes* also believed, Christianity, for Rousseau, is the history of men who gradually abandoned or finally misrepresented the teachings of its founder. Indeed, if Jesus himself

---

[1] Cf., *supra*, p. 31. Pierre Burgelin (*La Religion de Rousseau*, p. 42) sees a parallel between the 'Rousseau' who seeks 'Jean-Jacques' in the *Dialogues* and the Vicaire who seeks Jesus in the *Profession de foi*.

was unique as a person, his message was essentially rational and human in its emphasis. This is precisely what the Church has forgotten. The truth is that we should recognize 'a more than human virtue in his conduct' and 'a more than human wisdom in his lessons' (III. 698–9).

Rousseau's aversion to the idea of 'revelation' as a way to truth based on special powers and his reluctance to grant even Jesus any genuinely supernatural gifts are brought out very clearly in his attitude towards miracles. Many of the miracles recorded in the New Testament must belong to that category of 'things that are repugnant to reason' and the mind of 'any sensible man'. Rousseau believes that they can add nothing to the testimony of natural evidence, and may in fact merely confuse or repel those who are ready to respond to the simplicity and sublimity of the Gospels. Why should God need to have recourse to phenomena which run counter to the laws of the universe he has created, when the most impressive truth will always be 'the most common, the simplest, and the most reasonable'? Since our main ideas about God himself are based on nature alone, why should we need to invoke some supernatural authority to confirm them? This is the main burden of Rousseau's argument about miracles—that they are quite superfluous as supporting evidence for the truths of natural religion; they can add nothing to proofs based on the evidence of our 'eyes, judgement, and conscience'. In any case, to speak of the 'miraculous' quality of any phenomenon lying beyond our rational comprehension is surely to make a rash assumption, since it presupposes a complete knowledge of the laws of nature. According to Rousseau, the progress of science is constantly transforming alleged 'miracles' into commonplace events.

In the third of the *Lettres écrites de la Montagne*, which is devoted to a detailed examination of this problem, Rousseau tries to show that Jesus himself never used miracles to support the truth of his teaching; if he did perform them, as the New Testament says, it was never 'as a sign of his mission'; he categorically rejected the Jews' request that he should prove his divine authority by 'a sign from Heaven'. Similarly, modern Christians ought not to base their acceptance of religious doctrine on some allegedly miraculous proof that will seem merely useless or offensive to those who already believe in it on rational and moral grounds. Miracles will inevitably be an obstacle to any enlightened man's acceptance of Christianity. 'Remove the miracles from the Gospel and the whole earth will be at Jesus Christ's feet' (III. 735). At most, alleged miracles can convince simple people who are incapable of understanding the genuinely 'natural' basis of religion and in their case 'miracle' often means little more than 'superstition'.

Rousseau also stresses the great difficulty of distinguishing between true and false miracles, between miracles and *prestiges*. The Old Testament, for example, shows the magicians of Pharaoh's court performing the same miracles as Aaron; Moses' miracles were likewise imitated by his enemies. Even Jesus declared that false prophets would seek to deceive people with miracles and wonders. Since a miracle may apparently be the work of God or the Devil, Rousseau argues that it cannot stand by itself; its validity must be proved by the authority of the right doctrine. But this at once diminishes its significance, for 'if the doctrine is well founded, the miracle is superfluous, and if it is not, the doctrine can prove nothing' (III. 747). 'Thus after proving the doctrine by the miracle, it is necessary to prove the miracle by the doctrine, lest the work of the Devil be taken for the work of God' (*PF*. 335). Moreover, without this doctrinal support, the whole question may resolve itself into the purely factual and empirical one of deciding whether a specific event is a miracle or not, and this at once raises a problem to which no definite or permanent solution can be given.

After an apparently decisive rejection of miracles Rousseau qualifies his position in a characteristically conservative way. He recalls that his attitude towards miracles is essentially determined by their bearing upon religious experience rather than by any question of their possible truth or falsity. Whether miracles actually happen or not is unimportant, for they are superfluous as proofs of religious truth. More particularly, they cannot impinge on essential moral principles or man's fundamental attitude towards God. 'Je sers Dieu dans la simplicité de mon cœur. Je ne cherche à savoir que ce qui importe à ma conduite. Quant aux dogmes qui n'influent ni sur les actions ni sur la morale, et dont tant de gens se tourmentent, je ne m'en mets nullement en peine.' (*PF*. 417). This means in effect that Rousseau himself does not have to take a definite stand on the question of miracles. 'Non, monsieur, je ne les ai rejetés ni ne les rejette; si j'ai dit des raisons pour en douter, je n'ai point dissimulé les raisons d'y croire; il y a une grande différence entre nier une chose et ne la pas affirmer, entre la rejeter et ne pas l'admettre, et j'ai si peu décidé ce point, que je défie qu'on trouve un seul endroit dans tous mes écrits où je sois affirmatif contre les miracles' (III. 747). Since the whole issue has no relevance to man's ultimate moral and spiritual destiny, Rousseau considers that he can safely abandon himself to 'the involuntary scepticism' which is characteristic of his whole attitude towards questions lying beyond his immediate 'concern' or 'interest'. 'What matters to man is the fulfilling of his duties on earth.' Since miracles and wonders cannot help him to do this, they can be ignored with impunity. Nor need this involuntary scepticism be in any way 'painful', as long as man has taken a firm stand on 'the principles of all his duties'. The wisest attitude is therefore clear: 'Être toujours modeste et circonspect, mon enfant; respecter en silence ce qu'on ne saurait ni rejeter, ni comprendre, et s'humilier devant le grand être qui seul sait la vérité.' (*PF*. 415.)

5. *Religion and Society*

Convinced that man's spiritual needs can be fully satisfied through natural religion, Rousseau is suspicious of any Church which lays claim to special revelation and exclusive authority. Ecclesiastics, he believes, have no privileged access to truth. The problem of the Incarnation does not exist for Rousseau, and would in any case be eliminated by him as yet another obstacle in the way of man's immediate relationship with God; he does not accept the possibility of a particular sacramental mediation of divine grace and power. The Incarnation, he believes, is simply an occasion for the elaboration of futile theological subtleties. True religion, on the other hand, is characterized by a clarity and simplicity that appeal directly to man's mind and heart. As soon as they lose sight of this important truth and put their trust in authority, people become the victims of passion and prejudice as well as the instigators of hatred and intolerance. Organized religion, based on some supposedly unique claim to revelation, can lead only to a bigotry that sets men against one another, whereas natural religion brings them together in fraternal communion.

The variety of competing religious claims makes the discovery of truth a formidable and probably impossible task. Each of the three main religions of the western world—Judaism, Christianity, and Islam—bases its claim to allegiance on a supposedly infallible revelation. Truth is said to be embodied in a human authority endowed with supernatural powers. Yet, insists Rousseau, on looking more closely at the matter, we find that those very Christians who dispute so fiercely with one another about the claims of their own particular Churches, rarely understand the basis of other religions such as Judaism and Mohammedanism. Moreover, even supposing that they were prepared to seek the truth in good faith, how many men are qualified to undertake such complicated researches with any confidence? How many, for example, have the linguistic knowledge which would allow them to read the original texts? It is surely a question of initiating an investigation that is doomed to remain incomplete from the very outset. Natural religion, on the other hand, appeals to principles which every sincere man can find written in his own heart and mind 'in indelible characters'. Being permanent and universal, such principles are immediately accessible to every person of good faith; the conclusions of reason and conscience, confirmed by the voice of 'inner assent', possess a certainty and solidity which act as a precious safeguard against the bigotry of superstition and the waywardness of subjective caprice. This is brought out very clearly in the dialogue between 'le raisonneur' and 'l'inspiré' in the *Profession de foi*. True religion is based on unshakable rational principles which can never be impugned by endless disputes about historical evidence. The authority of men, as Rousseau tirelessly insists, can never be a substitute for 'the authority of God speaking to my reason'. 'Si les vérités éternelles que mon esprit conçoit pouvaient souffrir quelque atteinte, il n'y aurait plus pour moi nulle espèce de certitude' (*PF*. 357–9).

As for the two main forms of Christianity, Rousseau is personally more sympathetic to Protestantism than to Roman Catholicism. He peremptorily dismisses the claims of the Roman Church to occupy a unique and privileged place in Christian revelation on the grounds that they are based on a purely circular argument. 'The Church decides that the Church has the right to decide.' The apparently arbitrary basis of any authoritarian religion is inconsistent with Rousseau's conception of natural belief. The spirit of Roman Catholicism, in particular, repels him by its fanaticism and bigotry, the intolerance of its practices being equalled only by the irrationality of its doctrine. The idea that there is no salvation outside the Church is repugnant to both reason and nature. Like the *philosophes* Rousseau criticizes the unnatural and anti-social implications of the celibacy of the priesthood and of the whole monastic tradition. Protestantism, on the other hand, has the great merit of retaining certain 'natural' religious principles which, in Rousseau's view, make it more rational and more human in its appeal. 'Toute fausse religion combat la nature, la nôtre seule qui la suit et la rectifie annonce une constitution divine et convenable à l'homme' (II. 456).[1] This outlook is strengthened rather than inspired by the testimony of Scripture. 'J'ai vécu et je meurs', affirms the dying Julie, 'dans la communion protestante qui tire son unique règle de l'écriture sainte et de la raison.' She is thankful for having been brought up in 'une religion raisonnable et sainte qui, loin d'abrutir l'homme, l'ennoblit et l'élève, qui ne favorisant ni l'impiété ni le fanatisme, permet d'être sage et de croire, d'être humain et pieux tout à la fois' (II. 714, 724). The Vicaire undoubtedly expresses Rousseau's own views when he urges his young friend to return to a religion that is marked by the simplicity of reason and the purity of morality. 'Retournez dans votre patrie, reprenez la religion de vos pères, suivez-la dans la simplicité de votre cœur, et ne la quittez plus; elle est très simple et très sainte; je la crois de toutes les religions qui sont sur la terre celle dont la morale est la plus pure et dont la raison se contente le mieux' (*PF*. 439).

Rousseau's enthusiastic support of Protestantism was to be seriously affected by the embitterment of his relations with the Church of Geneva, and in the *Lettres écrites de la Montagne* of 1764 he accused the Genevans of having betrayed the true spirit of the Reformation. The polemical intention of this work perhaps led to some exaggeration of language, but there seems no valid reason for impugning the sincerity of Rousseau's views, even though in certain respects he may have misunderstood the Reformers' true intentions. Briefly, it would seem that he was too ready to adapt contemporary Protestantism to the requirements of his own 'natural' religion. With the rejection of the authority of the Roman

---

[1] Cf. also *Lettre à d'Alembert*: 'Toutes les fausses religions combattent la nature; la nôtre seule, qui la suit et la règle, annonce une constitution divine et convenable à l'homme' (ed. Fuchs, 171).

Church, argues Rousseau, the interpretation of religious principles, and especially of the Scriptures, must be undertaken by the individual himself with the help of his own reason. 'Voilà donc l'esprit particulier établi pour unique interprète de l'Écriture. Voilà l'autorité de l'Église rejetée; voilà chacun mis pour la doctrine sous sa propre jurisdiction' (III. 712). 'La raison particulière y prononce, en tirant la foi de la règle commune qu'elle établit, savoir l'Évangile.' The meaning of the Christian religion must therefore be freely interpreted by the individual without recourse to specific formulas or professions of faith. In fact, diversity of interpretation is a logical consequence of this position. The only interpretation that can be reasonably excluded is the one which seeks to exclude all others. Rousseau thus sees 'evangelical toleration' as the supreme principle of the Reformation. If it be objected that Calvin, who was 'undoubtedly a great man', did not admit this viewpoint, Rousseau replies that he was after all 'a man and, what is worse, a theologian'. 'He had, moreover, all the pride of the genius, which is aware of its superiority and is indignant that it should be contested' (III. 715). In the *Lettres écrites de la Montagne* Rousseau seems to retract the eulogy bestowed upon Calvin in the *Contrat social*. Moreover, Calvin's successors, who did not possess his genius, merely aggravated his mistakes by becoming polemical and intolerant in their turn—a development that merely shows how men can become the victims of their passions and prejudices even when they believe they are defending the truth. However, in Rousseau's opinion, the principles of the Reformation are the following: 'l'autorité de la raison en matière de foi, la libre interprétation des Écritures, la tolérance évangélique et l'obéissance aux lois, même en matière de culte; tous dogmes distinctifs et radicaux de l'Église Réformée, et sans lesquels, loin d'être solidement établie, elle ne pourrait pas même exister' (III. 719). As Rousseau's recent editors point out, this view of the Reformation is not historically tenable, for even though toleration is a consequence of Protestantism, the Reformed Churches have never seriously accepted the validity of a completely subjective interpretation of Christian dogmas.[1] However, having once established this initial premise, Rousseau can scarcely draw any other conclusion, for in his view Christianity at its best is little more than 'natural religion'. 'Le vrai christianisme', he declares,

[1] Cf. III. 1505; P. Burgelin, *La Religion de Rousseau*, p. 49.

'n'est que la religion naturelle mieux appliquée' (*CG.* VII. 329).

If Rousseau insists on calling himself a 'Christian', he does so in a way that deliberately dissociates him from the orthodox tradition. 'I am a Christian,' he tells the Archbishop of Paris, 'not as a disciple of priests, but as a disciple of Jesus Christ.' He claims to be following the truth of Jesus's teaching and refuses to identify himself with any precise theological conception of Jesus as God. As the supreme example of 'natural goodness', the spirit of Jesus does not need to be mediated through the Church, and Rousseau certainly allows no place for Christ the Redeemer, since his religious outlook excludes the idea of man's corruption through 'original sin'; natural goodness has been merely obscured or distorted through the nefarious influence of 'society', which, by 'depraving and perverting man', as Rousseau puts it in *Émile*, has become the source of all real evil.

As the supporter of natural religion, Rousseau believes that any attempt to express its universal content through precise verbal formulation will inevitably lead to a deterioration of spiritual quality. If he himself is a 'believer', it is not like *les gens à symboles et à formules*. True religious uniformity, he insists, lies in the heart and God must be worshipped 'in spirit and in truth'; 'this duty' belongs to 'all religions, all countries, all men'. No doubt each individual will have to apply the principles of natural religion to his own life, but the exact verbal expression of his beliefs is never important in itself; God is not interested in the individual's imperfect, halting attempts to convey his beliefs through language and thought, but in their effects upon his relations with his fellow men. The subjects which have been the source of bitter conflict between rival Christian churches are, in Rousseau's eyes, quite superficial: God is not concerned with 'the priest's garb, the order of words he uses, his gestures at the altar, or his genuflexions'. To attach importance to such matters is to create discord and controversy instead of that peace and harmony which should be the object of all true religion.

Curiously enough, although Rousseau at first sight seems to uphold a very radical and even revolutionary form of 'Christianity', he emerges ultimately as the defender of an ultra-conservative religious standpoint. Whereas one might have expected him to advocate a wholesale reform of the Christian Church (as Kierkegaard was to do, though for different reasons, a century later),

Rousseau argues for the retention of the *status quo*. In a word, he urges his fellow men to remain loyal to the religion of their forefathers, whether Protestant or Roman Catholic, and he never advised correspondents who consulted him on this subject to transfer their allegiance from one branch of the Christian Church to another. He seems to have accepted without difficulty the principle of *cuius regio eius religio*, according to which the sovereign had the right to fix the form of the national cult and require his subjects' obedience to it. If, therefore, the Vicaire savoyard exhorts his young friend to return to his forefathers' religion (Protestantism), he himself affirms his own intention of remaining loyal to his function as a priest in the Roman Church and of fulfilling this sacerdotal function with the utmost scrupulousness.

It may thus seem surprising to find a writer who lays such great stress on sincerity advocating an attitude which often suggests the very opposite, for is there not something disturbing in the idea of a man publicly attesting his allegiance to a religion in which he does not truly believe? How is it that the protagonist of 'natural religion' can become the defender of the most respectable religious orthodoxy? Rousseau himself was not at all worried by this apparent contradiction. In the first place, as we have seen, the Vicaire insists that certainty is possible only in questions which are of immediate interest to our personal existence, and that in matters which lie beyond our grasp the most sensible and prudent attitude is that of 'involuntary scepticism' or 'respectful doubt'. Although our reason is repelled (argues Rousseau) by the doctrine of the Trinity or the Biblical account of miracles, it would be unwise to reject such notions as absolutely untrue; it is far better to ignore them, since they have no bearing on the fulfilment of our moral obligations. A second and more practical reason for Rousseau's conservatism is to be found in his overriding concern with the unity and order of the State. Genuinely horrified by the thought of revolutionary conflict and civil strife, he opposes all activities which seem to threaten social peace. Since, in his opinion, nothing generates more passion and hatred than religious controversy, the sovereign is perfectly justified in treating such disputes as harmful to the public interest. Rousseau believes that no individual has the right to introduce a new religion into the country without the ruler's consent; although the latter ought to tolerate any religious minority that is already in existence, he can—and should—prevent the spread of new cults. Rousseau, therefore, favours the religion which commands the greatest number of adherents, for this seems likely to make for political and civil stability. Perhaps this explains the cool reception he gave to persecuted French Protestants who turned to him for help. Paradoxically, the French Roman Catholic Voltaire was to do more for this oppressed minority than the Genevan Protestant Rousseau!

In Rousseau's view, considerations of public order far outweigh any question of the truth or falsity of particular religious dogmas. The effectiveness of a national religion is to be determined by its ability to strengthen the unity and stability of the State rather than by its spiritual value; it is the social, not the religious function of the national cult which contributes to its real effectiveness. Rousseau is no doubt encouraged in this attitude by his conviction that the validity of doctrines lying outside the scope of natural religion can never be decided by rational argument. Since Christian dogmas, by the very fact of depending on revelation, will never command universal assent and are in any case irrelevant to morality, it does not matter very much which ones serve as the basis of the national religion provided that they do not foster civil discord. It is, in fact, the citizen's responsibility to infuse a truly religious spirit, that is, the spirit of 'natural' religion, into the national cult and so make it beneficial to the general welfare; religious beliefs, whatever their precise form, have positive value only when they help men to become better citizens and fulfil themselves as human beings. By giving a particular cult his approval and protection the ruler is simply acknowledging its social utility; if he insists upon imposing some uniformity of worship upon the citizens, this is simply as a means of preserving 'good order'; it is purely *une affaire de police* and does not imply any absolute approval of the religious cult as such. The ruler's primary concern, therefore, is to see that his subjects do not conduct themselves in an anti-social manner; he does not claim any jurisdiction over their private beliefs. Only when particular citizens try to impose their views on others is he forced to intervene. Rousseau insists that this attitude will contribute to the maintenance of order and yet leave the individual his religious freedom. On the one hand, nobody can be compelled to teach the principles of the national religion against his will, whilst, on the other, no citizen is forced to accept any particular doctrine or interpretation. 'Chacun en demeure seul juge pour lui-même, et ne reconnaît en cela d'autre autorité que la sienne propre' (III. 713). In Rousseau's opinion, this is precisely what his fellow Protestants have forgotten. As long as it does not involve an attitude of bigotry and intolerance, an individual's religion is his own affair.

The social emphasis of Rousseau's religious attitude is clearly revealed in his attitude towards the priesthood. A priest is not a privileged person by reason of some special spiritual gift or function conferred upon him by God, but simply because he is, in the abbé de Saint-Pierre's phrase which Rousseau quotes, 'un officier de morale'. The priest's value to the community is based on his unique opportunities for doing good to his fellow men. The function of the clergy, like that of the Church as a whole, should be to bring men closer together in brotherly love and to make them aware of their common human needs. Likewise, if Rousseau himself participates in the Holy Communion during his stay at Môtiers, it is because it allows him to establish a closer and more affectionate relationship with his 'brethren'. Any priest who maintains the intolerant doctrine that 'outside the Church there is no salvation' is betraying his true vocation by forgetting that a good priest is 'a minister of goodness, just as a good magistrate is a minister of justice'; his task should be to persuade his parishioners to love 'concord' and 'equality' and to practise the teaching of the Gospel, 'in which dogma is simple and morality sublime, in which we can see few religious practices and many works of charity'.

In spite of this attempt to assign a proper social role to Christianity, Rousseau realizes that the relations of Church and State involve great difficulties. The presence of any Christian Church in a community inevitably creates a tension and perhaps a conflict of loyalties in the hearts of its citizens; patriotism and Christianity seem to appeal to incompatible feelings, even when Christianity is interpreted, as in Rousseau's case, in a very liberal manner. The essential difficulty lies in the fact that patriotism is an inward-looking sentiment, concerned with a limited object, whilst Christianity directs itself outwards to humanity as a whole and to life in the next world. How can a religion, which is so exalted and spiritual in its ideals, be reconciled with the demands of a comparatively narrow outlook, concerned almost exclusively with the interest of a limited group of human beings? How can such a universal and other-worldly ideal help to strengthen feelings which are national and earthly in their emphasis? Whereas true Christianity would seem to have in view 'the universal social institution' which ignores all geographical and political frontiers, patriotism, like all earthly sentiments, must rely for its inspiration on the force of human passions. A national religion that is useful to the state would presumably by that very fact be prejudicial to the spiritual basis of Christianity. Conversely, it is difficult to imagine anything more 'contrary to the social spirit' than the Christian religion in its pure form; by teaching men to rise above their human passions and concentrate on heavenly rewards, it inevitably 'enervates' normal human emotions and weakens all attachment to finite things; by preaching 'servitude and dependence' it may actually prepare the way for tyranny and despotism. On the other hand, if the Church is given too much power, its intolerance creates strife and discord within the community. In short, if ideal Christianity is 'too sociable', contemporary Christian institutions are not sociable enough.

As Pierre Burgelin points out,[1] Rousseau never really solved this problem. However, the last chapter of the *Contrat social* recognizes the importance of religion as a social force and tries to overcome the difficulty in a rather different way. Admittedly, Rousseau is there more concerned with laying down *a priori* political principles than with drawing up practical plans for any particular community, and in this sense his solution is to a large extent abstract and utopian. Nevertheless, his ideas do go to the heart of the problem as he sees it and form a fitting conclusion to his discussion of the role of religion in society. It has been suggested that the chapter on civil religion in the *Contrat social* was something of an afterthought and did not form part of Rousseau's original purpose. This may well have been so, but the introduction of the religious theme into the work is proof of its importance for Rousseau's final evaluation of the political problem. In any case, it was in perfect conformity with his earlier thought. Already in *Émile* he had insisted upon the indissoluble link between morality and politics; religion served merely to make that link firmer and more specific. Even the idea of a 'civil religion' had been mentioned in his letter to Voltaire in 1756, and Rousseau had in fact urged his distinguished correspondent to devote his great talents to this very problem. The laws, he had then affirmed, can

[1] *La philosophie de l'existence de J.-J. Rousseau*, pp. 444–5.

impose 'a kind of profession of faith', although it is a purely negative one, except for its bearing on 'morality and natural right'. Negatively the State has the right to suppress any religion which 'attacks the foundations of society'. 'Je voudrais qu'on eût dans chaque état un code moral, une espèce de profession de foi civile qui contînt positivement les maximes sociales que chacun serait tenu d'admettre, et négativement les maximes fanatiques qu'on serait tenu de rejeter, non comme impies mais comme séditieuses. Ainsi, toute religion qui pourrait s'accorder avec le code serait admise, toute religion qui ne s'y accorderait pas serait proscrite, et chacun serait libre de n'en avoir point d'autre que le code même' (*Corresp. complete.* IV. 49). Such a civic profession of faith could serve as a bridge between religion and the State by satisfying the needs of both the individual and the citizen, for it would pay proper respect to humanity and patriotism. In this way, morality and civic obligation would be in complete accord. At the same time the citizen would be perfectly free to give his adherence to any religious beliefs that did not interfere with the performance of his civic duties. Nor need any serious conflict arise, because, in Rousseau's opinion, a man's personal religion has no need of external symbols; like all true 'natural' religion, it is 'without temples, altars, and rites' and is 'limited to the purely inward cult and the eternal obligations of morality'. Rousseau insists in the *Contrat social* that it may not improperly be called 'the pure and simple religion of the Gospel, true theism, and *le droit divin naturel*'.

An adequate civil religion, according to Rousseau, has two great advantages: it removes all contradiction and conflict from man's inner being, and simultaneously contributes to the unity and stability of the State. 'Tout ce qui rompt l'unité sociale ne vaut rien: toutes les institutions qui mettent l'homme en contradiction avec lui-même ne valent rien' (III. 464). The precise effect of a 'civil religion' will be to make a citizen 'love his duties', and this is possible because its dogmas are 'few and simple' and 'affirmed with precision, without explanations or commentaries'. 'The existence of a powerful, intelligent, beneficent, provident, and providing Divinity, the life to come, the happiness of the just, the punishment of the wicked, the sacredness of the Social Contract and the Laws; such are the positive dogmas. As for the negative dogmas, I limit them to a single one—intolerance' (III. 468-9).

Rousseau affirms that these dogmas are not meant to be 'religious' in the strict sense but *sentiments de sociabilité*. They express the principles of social morality raised, as it were, to a higher power.

From these principles Rousseau draws conclusions which have shocked modern liberal opinion, although they do not necessarily seem inconsistent with his own general outlook. He declares that any citizen who refuses to accept these doctrines will be banished from the state, but he will be banished as an unsociable and not as an impious man—in other words, as a man who has shown himself to be 'incapable of sincerely loving the laws and justice, and of sacrificing, if need be, his life to his duty'. Moreover, any citizen who, after giving his explicit assent to these doctrines, subsequently repudiates them will be punished by death, because he has committed 'the greatest of crimes: he has lied before the laws' (III. 468).

The reason for this apparent severity is not far to seek. Since, in Rousseau's view, the dogmas of civil religion form the inevitable basis of all genuine social morality, any man who refuses to accept them immediately violates the ethical basis of political life and so reveals himself as a criminal. Like so many predecessors and contemporaries—Plato and Locke, for example[1]—Rousseau does not think that the atheist can really be virtuous. In this respect he differs radically from the *philosophes*, but they perhaps are ahead of their day, whilst he is simply defending a more traditional and apparently more cautious standpoint. In any case, he sees no reason why any normal person should ever object to such ideas, since, in his view, they are an integral part of any social and political outlook which remains loyal to the principles of 'natural religion'.

[1] Cf. the editorial comments in III. 1505.

III

ROUSSEAU'S RELIGIOUS MYTHOLOGY

1. Paradise

ALTHOUGH the existential emphasis of Rousseau's religious thought related it closely to his own experience—he did not believe that a man had the right to teach other principles of whose truth he was not himself inwardly, even passionately, convinced—it was never a question of simply transposing subjective feelings into philosophical ideas; he recognized that the value of his own religious experience, which was in many ways restricted and incomplete, depended on the influence of an ideal self that belonged to man in general rather than to any particular individual. No doubt the idealistic possibilities of human nature portrayed in Rousseau's writings were partly inspired by a personal need, for the contemplation of a perfect world helped him to escape from the limitations of his everyday existence, but he did not believe that this was a mere idiosyncrasy of his own; he was convinced that his vision of perfection was a noble ideal, worthy of all men of good faith.

Because it represented an intimate part of his personal experience as well as a universal ideal, perfection did not remain for Rousseau a simple abstraction, but inspired an active search for 'supreme felicity'. Perfect happiness had to be an experience that was both immediate and absolute—the self's active realization of all its authentic possibilities and the enjoyment of 'all the felicity of which it felt itself capable' (I. 822). To achieve this goal was an extremely difficult task, requiring an exceptional coincidence of mood, time, and circumstances. How few people were privileged to enjoy this supreme experience! Only on rare occasions did Rousseau himself believe that he had found complete happiness, perhaps the most outstanding of these being the experience of reverie and the pure 'feeling of existence' on the Île de Saint-Pierre. In spite of being 'intoxicated' with 'perfections of every kind', he was compelled to acknowledge that absolute felicity remained a haunting possibility rather than a genuine reality of everyday life.

Since true happiness was rarely attainable in the ordinary world,

Rousseau sought it constantly in some form of contemplation. The felicity which was not vouchsafed to him on earth could only be discovered in those 'ethereal regions' where 'the pleasure of existing' was encountered in all its perfection. Even in his youthful years he had tended to find satisfaction in silent contemplation rather than restless activity, and in later life he was more and more inclined to treat 'eternal leisure' as the essential condition of the paradisaic existence, whether in this life or the next (I. 640). Typical of this mood was his happiness with Madame de Warens: 'J'étais dans un calme ravissant, jouissant sans savoir de quoi. . . . Je me taisais, je la contemplais, et j'étais le plus heureux des hommes' (I. 107). Rousseau thought that, unlike *l'homme intéressé*, who was more concerned with 'multiplying the instruments of enjoyment' than with enjoyment itself, the truly happy man did not wish to possess but to *be*, and that it was especially in the mood of contemplation that he could become fully aware of the reality of his own existence.

Nevertheless, Rousseau admitted that since contemplation often became a substitute for the disappointments of everyday life, it was not usually found in its pure form. The god-like self-sufficiency of reverie being a comparatively rare occurrence, it was sometimes necessary to 'animate' an 'abstract and monotonous reverie' with 'charming images'. In other words, contemplation required the help of the imagination to give it specific shape and substance. Moreover, the inclusion of sensuous images in the dream of perfection forced Rousseau to have recourse to memories of his own past life, of those brief periods when complete happiness seemed to be within his grasp. Even though these memories were transmuted and idealized through the activity of his imagination, they were still rooted in earthly desires, so that his 'sublime' and 'ravishing contemplations' contained both mundane and ideal elements. In general, however, his persistent preoccupation with the dream of perfection and his growing tendency to attribute absolute value to these moods caused him to treat them as a kind of religious experience. He believed that at such times he was being granted a glimpse of paradise.

The theme of paradise was a particularly significant aspect of Rousseau's imaginative life, for it constantly impelled him towards 'another world', a 'new world' freed from the imperfections of ordinary life. This 'ideal world' appeared in moments of inspiration and exaltation when a dazzling 'illumination' carried him up to a higher realm of being. As a writer, he believed he had been called upon to offer his fellow men the vision of 'another moral world' and 'another intellectual world'; the 'sudden inspiration' on the road to Vincennes marked the beginning of his literary vocation by revealing the existence of 'another universe'. On more carefree occasions when he was able to enjoy the exhilaration of his delightful journeys on foot, he saw himself as 'the master of the whole of nature' with 'a new paradise waiting for him at the door' (I. 163). Saint-Preux was undoubtedly echoing his creator's experience when, among the Alps, he was able to 'observe in some way another nature and find himself in a new world' (II. 79). Such ecstatic moments were often associated not only with the vision of a perfect world but also with a transformation of personal existence. As soon as he read the subject of the prize-essay in the *Mercure de France*, Rousseau 'saw another universe and became another man' (I. 351); his soul then began to burn with a 'celestial fire' as he 'became another and ceased to be himself' (I. 416–17). In his last years, when he believed he was the victim of universal persecution, he considered himself to be 'the inhabitant of another sphere in which nothing resembles this one' (I. 934).

Although it represented the satisfaction of Rousseau's most ardent longings, paradise was not a solitary place, for it allowed him to enjoy the companionship of the ideal beings created by his imagination—of those 'people of another world' who experienced a form of happiness that anticipated the bliss of the next life. In another favourite expression this new world of the imagination was a 'true golden age'. Likewise, the happy days of man's past, when he had achieved an awareness of himself as a human being and was still ignorant of the evils of civilization, constituted 'a golden age' that was also humanity's 'happiest and most durable period', 'the real youth of the world' (II. 171). Rousseau enjoyed a similar feeling of idyllic contentment in his personal life whenever he was free to follow his bent and imagine himself to be living with ideal companions amid the beauties of nature; there he was able to create 'a golden age *à sa fantaisie*' (I. 1140).

Although Rousseau's vision of paradise assumes a number of different forms, its unity and coherence are assured by the persistence of certain essential features. As we have already seen from his emphasis upon 'supreme felicity', paradise is the place where man finds complete personal fulfilment and is truly himself in all his perfection; in paradise he is 'fully himself, without diversion and without obstacle'. If his life with Madame de Warens seemed so enchanting to Jean-Jacques, it was because with her he had been 'fully himself, without admixture and without obstacle'. As he explains in the eighth Promenade of the *Rêveries*, he is 'the happiest of mortals' in the 'earthly paradise' of nature, because he not only believes himself to be beyond the reach of his enemies, but also because he is 'happy and content, without diversion, without obstacle'. On such occasions he feels he has overcome all inner tension and contradiction and freed himself from all external hindrances. To be in paradise is to achieve absolute personal unity in an environment that allows the spontaneous and untrammelled enjoyment of the self's deepest possibilities; happiness is inseparable from complete and immediate satisfaction with one's own being, a satisfaction that is 'independent of fortune and events'. Since true felicity lies beyond the range of normal thought and language and the desire to seek material things, the 'art of enjoyment' is incompatible with 'the torment of possession'; it consists entirely of the pleasure of *being*.

In paradise, then, existence is an end in itself, because it is a state that knows nothing of the weaknesses and imperfections of daily life. More specifically, it means the recovery of complete innocence and the attainment of absolute purity. This is indeed one of the most persistent and fundamental aspects of Rousseau's dream of perfect happiness. His own hope of immortality is based in no small measure on the conviction that, in spite of all his shortcomings, he has never lost his original innocence, and that one day he will be found worthy to experience it afresh in all its purity. Nowhere is this more clearly revealed than in his portrait of himself in the *Dialogues* as the 'man of nature' who has never ceased to be an 'elderly child'. Such wrongs as he has committed can be explained, he believes, by the pernicious influence of 'society', which has temporarily alienated him from his true self and made him a victim of prejudice and 'false shame'; within himself he knows that 'no evil thought has ever approached his heart' and that no man is 'better' than he. His sins are sins of omission, not commission; he has never been guilty of deliberate wickedness. In paradise, whether in heaven or on earth, innocence appears as the supreme quality which sustains all the rest.

To attain complete innocence man has to cast aside the burden of his guilty past and begin life anew. To regain his innocence he has to be reborn. This is another important theme in Rousseau's description of paradise, although it is often given indirect and symbolical expression. In certain exceptional circumstances he himself experienced a strangely satisfying sense of rebirth.[1] Such was the case with the unusual accident at Menilmontant in 1776, when he was knocked down by a large dog. On regaining consciousness, he was in a curiously euphoric state of amnesia, in which the loss of memory was accompanied by a heightened feeling of existence, but of an expansive feeling that was bereft of any genuine awareness of personal identity. 'Je naissais dans cet instant à la vie, et il me semblait que je remplissais de ma légère existence tous les objets que j'apercevais. Tout entier au moment présent je ne me souvenais de rien; je n'avais nulle notion distincte de mon individu, pas la moindre idée de ce qui venait de m'arriver; je ne savais ni qui j'étais ni où j'étais; je ne sentais ni mal, ni crainte, ni inquiétude' (I. 1005). He seemed to be living through an experience which had overcome all the normal limitations of time and space as well as the fears and anxieties of his inner life; in his whole being he felt 'a ravishing calm' that exceeded the satisfaction derived from all known pleasures. Marcel Raymond compares this description with the passage in *Les Solitaires* (the projected sequel to *Émile*) where it is stated that for a man to be happy he has 'to drink the waters of oblivion and put himself in the condition of somebody who is *beginning to live*' (I. 1774). Somewhat similar was the 'happy revolution' which took place in Julie's soul at the time of her marriage to M. de Wolmar. 'I believed that I could feel myself being reborn; I believed that I was again beginning another life' (II. 355): only in this way could she hope to free herself from the memory of her guilty passion and recover her 'primitive character'. Henceforth she would be 'a new being recently come forth from nature's hands' (II. 364). The notion of rebirth was thus linked with the idea of the re-creation of 'nature' and the acquisition of 'a new being' freed from all the guilt of its previous existence.

The same concern with the innocence of rebirth is present in

---

[1] See also on this theme the important article by B. Munteano, 'La Solitude de Rousseau', *Annales Jean-Jacques Rousseau*, XXXI (1946–9), esp. p. 166.

some of Rousseau's reactions to natural phenomena. Of all the seasons of the year he prefers the spring, the time when the earth is reborn and life begins to stir anew. As he puts it in an eloquent sentence of the *Confessions*, 'for me to see the spring again was to be resurrected in paradise' (I. 233). In the second book of *Émile*, he affirms that 'when you see the rebirth of nature, you feel that you yourself are being restored to life'. In the same way, Jean-Jacques was always a man of the dawn, the hour which heralds the birth of a new day and the re-emergence of a new zest for life; it was at this time that his prayer to God was the most fervent, his love of nature most intense. 'When I got up', he told Malesherbes, 'before the sun in order to go and watch it rise in my garden, and when I saw a fine day beginning, my first wish was that neither letters nor visits would come to disturb its charm' (I. 1139).[1] At such a moment he could establish direct contact with the beauties of 'the whole of nature and its inconceivable author'.

The discovery of innocence was inseparable from a wonderful feeling of simplicity. In this respect his imagination was faithful to one of the most fundamental aspects of his intellectual outlook. Innocence and purity always involved a simplification of existence and the elimination of all 'subtlety' and 'mystery', although this betokened a great enrichment, not an impoverishment of being—the achievement of an absolute plenitude. Simplicity and innocence suggested also the idea of light and transparence.[2] For Rousseau paradise always had a translucent quality which made it a worthy abode for God's creatures.

Innocence and light are also the source of yet another essential characteristic of paradise—peace. Both innocence and peace are essential to an existence 'without division and obstacle'. The 'ravishing calm' of the Ménilmontant episode was not the least remarkable of its features. It is, therefore, not surprising that the earthly paradise of Clarens should reflect 'the peace of the celestial abode'. Only when the soul is at peace can it truly enjoy the plenitude and transparence of its own being.

Furthermore, the attainment of innocence and peace is possible

---

[1] Cf. I. 135, for a brief but vivid description of another dawn—of the summer day of his idyllic encounter with Mlle de Graffenried and Mlle Galley.

[2] This theme has been brilliantly developed by Jean Starobinski in his remarkable book, *Jean-Jacques Rousseau, la transparence et l'obstacle* (Paris, 1957).

because in paradise the problem of earthly time no longer exists. Whereas finite man is tormented by regret for the past or anxiety for the future, being always 'behind' or 'ahead' of himself, so that the happiness of a perfectly stable, unchanging state seems a mere chimera, the enjoyment of paradise overcomes all temporal divisions. Time is not abolished, but fulfilled in the form of eternity; but this eternity is of a special kind, for it takes the form of an 'eternal present'. The three dimensions of earthly time are reduced to one that contains the essence of them all, and the whole content of existence is given a new, intense immediacy. Already a particularly happy moment of this earthly life can give a foretaste of the bliss that is to come. After describing the days which formed 'the true happiness of his life', days spent amid the beauties of nature, Rousseau tells Malesherbes that he would willingly exist for ever in this way. 'Yes, monsieur, may such days fill eternity for me' (I. 1142). The feeling of having discovered an eternal present is one of the most memorable aspects of the state of reverie. Having observed that the 'continual flux' of life on earth provides very few moments of which it can be truly said that one 'would like them to last for ever', since even the most intense happiness ultimately leaves our heart 'anxious and empty', Rousseau insists that reverie is a mode of being in which 'time does not exist for the soul, and the present always endures without marking its duration and without any trace of succession, without any other feeling of privation or enjoyment, of pleasure or pain, of desire or fear, than that of our existence alone, and this feeling is sufficient to fill it completely' (I. 1046). In conditions like these the soul enjoys a 'full, perfect, and sufficient happiness' which makes it 'self-sufficient like God'.

Because of these various qualities, paradisaic existence involves a remarkable enhancement of personal consciousness, a 'new elevation' which lifts up the soul into the 'ethereal regions'. Paradise, therefore, is not empty solitude, but a state of absolute unity and plenitude that transcends all the limitations of earthly life while fulfilling all its finest potentialities. Moreover, one of the most satisfying attributes of human consciousness is its capacity for the enjoyment of beauty. Innocence, light, transparence, peace, and plenitude require the presence of beauty to make them complete. Rousseau insists that perfect happiness involves a 'sublimity' inspired by the contemplation of beauty. 'The soul's true enjoyment is in the contemplation of beauty' (II. 224). His own 'sweetest meditations' are those of 'order, harmony, beauty, perfection' (I. 824). A man as enamoured of ideals as Jean-Jacques can scarcely be indifferent to the beauty of perfection. 'Idolâtre du beau dans tous les genres, resterait-il froid uniquement pour la suprême beauté? Non. Elle ornera de ses charmes immortels ces images chéries qui remplissent son âme, qui repaissent son cœur'. This is perhaps not unexpected when we recall that in Rousseau's eyes goodness and beauty were not two distinct values, but two facets of the same spiritual reality, the good being merely the beautiful 'put into action'. In paradise all fundamental values become one and constitute a single absolute experience.

Since God is the ultimate source of all values, the beautiful order created by him will inevitably fire the soul with a 'sacred enthusiasm'. Attention has already been called to the importance of order in Rousseau's religious thought[1] and the particular satisfaction which man can obtain from identifying himself with the 'universal system'. In paradise the beauty of this order will become even more evident as it is imbued with a vividness and an intensity that fill with ecstasy a being noteworthy for its innocence and plenitude. 'The sublime contemplations' of an earthly paradise, reinforced by the activity of an imagination that is 'rich in pleasant scenes', will take the form of 'celestial visions' that delight and ravish the soul.

The 'supreme felicity' of the true paradise can, of course, be enjoyed only in the next life, and Rousseau, in his last years, dwells more and more on the idea of immortality as a state of being in which the self, free and perfected, will at last be admitted to the chosen company of the 'celestial intelligences' (I. 1049, 1142). In this earthly life, on the other hand, the absolute bliss of paradise can be glimpsed on only a few privileged occasions when the self seems to enjoy an experience of indescribable perfection. For the most part man's 'sublime contemplations' are less ethereal, the mere presence of the imagination necessarily giving paradise a certain shape and substance. However celestial and idealized its ultimate form, the perfect world of the imagination has to possess some features which recall the joys of earthly existence. To an ordinary man the beauty of paradise is inconceivable without a sensuous element, and the principle of order itself presupposes a

[1] Cf., *supra*, p. 48.

certain degree of limitation, for the universal system created by God possesses a structure that makes it accessible to man's perception. Rousseau's vision of paradise, therefore, takes the form of *le paradis terrestre*, of a paradise in which human elements are imbued with an eternal quality, perfect and yet imperfect, ideal and yet real, spiritual and yet physical. The earthly content of his imaginative vision is transformed through the idealizing power of spiritual aspirations, which help to shape and transform the situations and characters thus evoked, and so provide the basis of a religious 'mythology'.

The earthly paradise, then, does not consist of a merely vague yearning for the infinite or a confused longing for immortality, but assumes the form of a finite world, with recognizable characteristics and yet containing the essential qualities of innocence, transparence, peace, simplicity, and beauty. It is not a world of absolute solitude or infinite expansion, but as previous critics have already observed (and Amiel, among the first), Rousseau's ideal is a perfect island.[1] It will be recalled that he sometimes spoke of spending his last years on an island like Cyprus or Majorca, whilst the supreme happiness of reverie was experienced on the Île de Saint-Pierre. Significantly too, one of his favourite characters was Robinson Crusoe, the man who became the self-sufficient monarch of a desert island he had made his own. Rousseau's chosen habitation was 'a fertile and lonely island, naturally circumscribed and separated from the rest of the universe' (hence the importance of the ocean) and yet offering 'the companionship of a small number of inhabitants'. 'Why cannot I go and end my days in this beloved island without ever leaving it?' (I. 1048) The influence of this ideal upon Rousseau's imagination is also shown in a curiously inverted manner in another context: in moments of despair he hoped to find refuge in voluntary imprisonment, a prison, with its walls and circumscribed space, being a more sombre and restricted form of the same insular ideal. A similar preoccupation also emerges in a more symbolical way in his dream of living in a small, self-contained community cut off from the rest of the world. Such was the society of Clarens, Rousseau's most elaborate imaginative attempt to create paradise on earth, for this community was like a

---

[1] Cf. also an interesting chapter in M. Eigeldinger, *Jean-Jacques Rousseau et la réalité de l'imaginaire* (Neuchâtel, 1962), Ch. IV, 'L'âge d'or est insulaire'.

self-contained island cut off from the rest of the world and content to live on its own resources and pleasures.

Not unnaturally, perhaps, the creation of an ideal world capable of satisfying his overriding love of perfection led Rousseau to recall those moments of his life—and of the life of humanity too—when innocence and peace seemed to reign on earth. As the world grew darker and more menacing, he looked back with ever greater pleasure upon what he believed to be the idyllic years of his early childhood, when, as he says in the *Confessions*, he really lived in 'an earthly paradise'. Primitive man too, in Rousseau's eyes, was a being who enjoyed the same kind of happiness—the happiness of a being completely identified with 'the feeling of his existence'; neither the child nor the primitive man needs to go beyond what he immediately is, for each is content to enjoy his own being. Like all the inhabitants of paradise, these simple creatures are innocent, peaceful, and almost self-sufficient inasmuch as they do not seek resources beyond themselves; and yet they live in perfect harmony with a physical environment which appears capable of satisfying all their desires.

Attractive though it may be in so many ways, the paradise of childhood and primitive man falls short of perfection in certain essential respects. In the first place, its innocence and simplicity are of a predominantly instinctive, almost animal-like kind, without any genuine self-consciousness; if the child and primitive man are happy, they are happy without reflection; they have a primordial, rudimentary mode of existence, and are faithful to its own inherent possibilities but without any explicit understanding of its true quality. From this point of view it is quite correct to say with Rousseau in the *Discours sur l'origine de l'inégalité* that 'the man who meditates is a depraved animal', since reflection violates the simplicity and unity of this immediate and spontaneous mode of being. In the second place, childhood represents an ideal located in the past, one which, once abandoned, is irrecoverable; although the adult may like to invest this phase of his life with a static, timeless quality, he knows that it could never have stayed the same for ever; even the child possesses possibilities and 'virtual capacities' which destine him sooner or later to move on to a more complex and developed phase of existence. The same limitation is also apparent in mankind as a whole. Although, unlike the child, humanity, in Rousseau's opinion, might have remained in a permanently primitive state, the advent of society—perhaps the result of a 'fatal chance' and fortuitous physical circumstances—means that man has reached a stage of historical development which makes it impossible for him to return to his original innocence. 'Human nature never moves backwards and people never go back to the age of innocence and equality when they have once moved away from it' (I. 935).

The paradise of primitive man is defective in yet one other serious respect: it is the life of a self-sufficient but isolated being who, because he does not form any permanent attachments to others, never attains any moral consciousness. Solitude is in a sense a condition of his happiness, since it is the lack of complex relationships which enables him to preserve his simplicity and innocence. Being satisfied, for example, with brief sexual encounters, he knows nothing of the torment of civilized 'love', but he is also ignorant of its sublime possibilities; if he is oblivious of the modern man's fear of death, he is also without thought of immortality. Morally speaking, he is neither good nor bad: he is 'nothing'. On the other hand, Rousseau's dream of paradise with its 'happy fictions' and 'delightful visions' requires the presence of 'beings after his own heart'. 'Laissant concourir ses sens à ses fictions, il se forme des êtres selon son cœur, et vivant avec eux dans une société dont il se sent digne, il plane dans l'empyrée au milieu des objets charmants et presque angéliques dont il s'est entouré' (I. 858). This idea of a 'loving heart' in search of ideal affection is a theme to which he returns again and again. His fictions, he declares, are not those of a misanthropic character, but of a man 'devoured by the need to love'. Indeed, this craving for perfect love provides one of the main reasons for his belief in immortality. Forced to endure isolation and misunderstanding on earth, his 'expansive soul' still clings to the hope of finding affection in another realm of being. 'Tous ses malheurs ne vinrent que de ce besoin d'aimer qui dévora son cœur dès son enfance et qui l'inquiète et le trouble encore au point que, resté seul sur la terre, il attend le moment d'en sortir pour voir réaliser enfin ses visions favorites, et retrouver dans un meilleur ordre de choses une patrie et des amis' (I. 827). In spite of a superficial resemblance between his situation and that of 'the man of nature', Jean-Jacques, primitive man can clearly know nothing of such an ideal. Childhood, on the other hand, offers better opportunities for the establishment of close friendships.

Rousseau recalls with emotion his own happy intimacy with his cousin, Abraham Bernard, at Bossey. As they lived beneath the benevolent gaze of their guardians, the two children seemed to be in 'the earthly paradise'. 'Always inseparable, we were sufficient for each other' (I. 25–6).[1] Yet by its very nature this blissful state could not last, and soon, with the episode of the broken comb, the child Jean-Jacques had to know the harshness of a world that sacrificed innocence to injustice. Even if the human being could retain the child's naïveté, he would still fall short of perfect happiness. Childhood, like the life of primitive man, is a stage of existence which is by its very nature transitory and irrecoverable.

A third and perhaps more promising kind of paradise is that of 'first love'. Rousseau stresses repeatedly that the perfect companion of his dreams has to be a woman rather than a man; although sexual differences do not count in the heavenly state, his earthly paradise requires the presence of the ideal woman. Moreover, Rousseau's perfect woman always possesses that mysterious quality of innocence which is essential to the inhabitants of paradise. The actual facts of his passion for Madame d'Houdetot do not leave an impression of unsullied purity, but it was precisely this aspect of their relationship which stood out most clearly in his memory in later years. 'L'éclat de toutes les vertus ornait à mes yeux l'idole de mon cœur; en souiller la divine image eût été l'anéantir' (I. 444). He liked to believe that his love was so idealistic that it excluded all idea of physical possession. 'I loved her too much to want to possess her' (I. 444). The 'pure feelings' of two hearts united in the 'delightful effusion' of intimacy could not know unworthy desires. Although this amorous episode was often more banal and sordid than Rousseau's account suggests, it was transformed with the passing of time into an 'immortal memory of innocence and enjoyment'.

It was especially in the still freer atmosphere of literary creation that Rousseau's imagination could produce the most entrancing picture of first love. In the idyllic phase of their early love Julie and Saint-Preux find the bliss of a self-sufficient paradise. As Julie, to whom this ideal is particularly attractive, says, 'the accord of love and innocence seem to me to be paradise on earth' (II. 51). She now feels great 'happiness and peace reigning in the depths of her soul' because 'the charms of the union of hearts are joined to those

---

[1] Cf., *supra*, p. 4.

of innocence'. For her nothing is more precious than 'the serenity of an innocent soul'. When later on she nostalgically recalls their early love, she dwells on its self-sufficient and peaceful character, the close and quiet intimacy of two people who need nobody else to make their love complete. 'Our hearts were sufficient for each other.' In his very last pages Rousseau recalls a similar happiness with Madame de Warens. 'Oh! if I had been sufficient for her heart as she was sufficient for mine!' (I. 1098.) Once again this self-sufficient kind of paradise emerges as a state of being rather than possession. Erotic desire seems to be stilled as the two lovers achieve a perfect equilibrium of innocence and affection. Yet this paradise, like the others, cannot endure, because adolescent love is but one stage in the development of a fuller and richer experience. In spite of its appearance of utter peace the force of erotic feeling will ultimately involve Saint-Preux and Julie in a tormented relationship subject to all the vicissitudes of time. As Jean-Jacques was to learn, the desire of the young impels them away from innocence and tranquillity towards the world of conflict and guilt. Although the ageing Rousseau looked back upon his life with Mme de Warens as a perfect idyll, his vision of the past represented an old man's yearning for what might have been rather than a faithful memory of what had really existed.

Rousseau seems to admit that these three forms of paradise cannot satisfy all the demands of his imagination. As he becomes involved in the difficulties and contradictions of adult life, he realizes that the persistent longing for innocence and simplicity, however spiritual in essence, has to make some concession to physical human reality. Though apparently simple and absolute, the supreme felicity of existence remains the idealized expression of a number of different personal desires which involve his reactions to people and things as well as his yearning for ideal bliss. His 'fictions' are not those of a solitary man completely cut off from the world but of one who, in spite of his solitude, still desires to bring himself into closer contact with the universal system of which he forms part. Merely subjective feeling has to be enriched by the presence of images drawn from external reality, or, as Jean-Jacques puts it, his 'fictions' require the 'concourse of his senses'.

Perhaps the most striking difference between the paradise of the adult and the more naïve world of childhood and primitive man is the way in which the former combines highly developed personal feeling with an active appreciation of its dependence upon the beauty of the physical environment, but the latter lacks any definite awareness of its true value and meaning. True paradise, on the other hand, is based on the intimate fusion of individual emotion and sense-experience. This is very apparent in Rousseau's description of his idyllic life with Madame de Warens. 'I saw her everywhere among the flowers and verdure; her charms and those of spring were intermingled' (I. 105). The enhancement of personal emotion is accompanied by a transfiguration of the external world which is thereby made more vivid and beautiful. After describing his ability to 'enjoy the present' and share in 'quiet pleasures' which had 'the serenity of paradise', he relates how, during one blissful walk with *Maman*, the whole of nature appeared to be transformed. 'Tout semblait conspirer au bonheur de cette journée. Il avait plu depuis peu; point de poussière, et des ruisseaux bien courants. Un petit vent frais agitait les feuilles, l'air était pur, l'horizon sans nuages; la sérénité régnait au Ciel comme dans nos cœurs' (I. 244).[1] Both the physical landscape and the hearts of the two happy persons in its midst were filled with innocence, peace, and transparence. The physical and the human worlds became imbued with the same paradisaic qualities.

Saint-Preux experiences a similar ecstatic transformation of his own being and the outside world. Amid the Alps he feels himself to be participating in a 'magical' and 'supernatural' scene; uplifted by the 'unalterable purity' of the mountain air, his meditations assume a 'great' and 'sublime' character, whilst his deep love for Julie makes nature's sensuous beauty seem much more intense and impressive. 'Je trouve la campagne plus riante, la verdure plus fraîche et plus vive, l'air plus pur, le ciel plus serein; le chant des oiseaux semble avoir plus de tendresse et de volupté; le murmure des eaux inspire une langueur plus amoureuse; la vigne en fleurs exhale au loin de plus doux parfums; un charme secret embellit tous les objets ou fascine mes sens . . .'. Having observed that these 'adornments of spring' require the presence of two faithful lovers to make them complete, Saint-Preux cries out ecstatiquement: 'Allons animer toute la nature, elle est morte sans les feux de l'amour' (II. 116–17). Nor is it merely erotic love which is capable of producing

[1] Cf. J. Starobinski, op. cit., p. 99, for a commentary on similar passages as expressions of Rousseau's desire for transparence and openness.

this transformation. In the *Confessions* Rousseau points out that the delights of reverie can have a similar effect. 'Le concours des objets sensibles rend ses méditations moins sèches, plus douces, plus illusoires, plus appropriées à lui tout entier. La nature s'habille pour lui des formes les plus charmantes, se peint à ses yeux des couleurs les plus vives, se peuple pour son usage d'êtres selon son cœur' (I. 816). Finally, in the ideal world described at the beginning of the first of the *Dialogues*, 'a world that is like ours and yet quite different', there occurs a similar enhancement of sense-experience.

La nature y est la même que sur notre terre, mais l'économie en est plus sensible, l'ordre en est plus marqué, le spectacle plus admirable; les formes sont plus élégantes, les couleurs plus vives, les odeurs plus suaves, tous les objets plus intéressants. Toute la nature y est si belle que sa contemplation enflammant les âmes d'amour pour un si touchant tableau leur inspire avec le désir de concourir à ce beau système la crainte d'en troubler l'harmonie, et delà naît une exquise sensibilité qui donne à ceux qui en sont doués des jouissances immédiates, inconnues aux cœurs que les mêmes contemplations n'ont pas avivés (I. 668).

Here we can observe transposed into a sensuous key several of the 'paradise' themes already analysed—innocence, purity, beauty, spontaneity, but if existence becomes purer and more translucent, it also acquires greater vividness and intensity. These qualities are now able to give 'immediate enjoyment' and 'kindle' the soul, because they form part of a greater reality—of a harmonious system remarkable for its beauty and sublimity. Nature in the broadest sense is no longer a mere agglomeration of particular elements, but an ordered system with a spiritual and sensuous appeal that not only testifies to its supernatural origin but also attracts the human soul directly.

The close link between Rousseau's emotional needs and his feeling for nature prevents him from seeing the world in a merely physical way, even though the senses help to give it form and beauty. At its best his sensibility always contains, in his own word, a 'moral' element, that is, an element which is more dependent on his heart than on his senses. Some of his most characteristic reactions to nature owe more to emotional than to physical needs; he often looks to nature for the solace he has sought in vain from human beings. More especially he likes to treat her as a comforting maternal presence. The persistence of this maternal theme throughout Rousseau's work has induced at least one critic to interpret it as a search for the ideal mother.[1] Although, as we shall see, this is in fact only one aspect of a complex mood, it certainly expresses a very profound inner need. Rousseau feels a kind of umbilical tie with this great 'mother' who can protect him against adversity. He rarely fails to be comforted by 'the tender care of the common mother' (the phrase is Julie's (II. 113)); or, as Jean-Jacques puts it in the second of the *Dialogues*, 'the countryside itself would be less charming in his eyes if he did not see in it the solicitude of the common mother who delights to adorn her children's abode' (I. 807). When, on the Île de Saint-Pierre, he was savouring the delights of reverie, he could not help crying out from time to time; 'O nature, O mother, here I am under your sole protection; here no cunning, villainous men can come between you and me' (I. 644). In the seventh Promenade he explains how 'taking refuge with the common mother, he sought in her arms to escape from the assaults of her children' (I. 1066). Mother-nature, therefore, provided him with a sense of immediate security in a hostile human world.

Perhaps this preoccupation with the universal common mother explains another characteristic physical reaction of symbolical significance—Rousseau's love of water. Although it is not part of our present purpose to discuss the validity of the well-known psychoanalytical interpretation of water as a mother-symbol, it is worth recording that Rousseau himself rarely fails to include a lake in his description of an earthly paradise. Moreover, the insular ideal to which reference has already been made presupposes the proximity of a vast ocean which shuts him off from the rest of the world and at the same time gives him a sense of self-sufficient security. Recalling in the *Confessions* the emotions aroused by the sight of the region of Vaud, he says: 'Quand l'ardent désir de cette vie heureuse et douce qui me fuit et pour laquelle j'étais né vient enflammer mon imagination, c'est toujours au pays de Vaud, près du lac, dans des campagnes charmantes qu'elle se fixe. Il me faut absolument un verger au bord de ce lac et non pas d'un autre; il me faut un ami sûr, une femme aimable, une vache et un petit bateau. Je ne jouirai d'un bonheur parfait sur la terre que quand j'aurai tout cela' (I. 152). Clearly this dream owes much to the memory of his childhood, but it also expresses a strong adult need

[1] Cf. E. Gilliard, *De Rousseau à Jean-Jacques* (Lausanne, 1950).

—the need for affection, peace, and security. On another occasion he made a special point of returning to Lausanne because 'he wanted to feast upon the sight of this beautiful lake which can there be seen in its greatest extent' (I. 146). He also relates in the *Confessions* how the earthly paradise of *La Nouvelle Héloïse* has to be completed by the presence of a particular lake, Lac Léman. The perfect reverie described in the fifth *Promenade* is achieved on a lake whose waters 'lull' his eyes and ears with their quiet rhythm. When the weather is not suitable for boating, he likes to sit down in some lonely spot 'in order to gaze at the superb and enchanting sight of the lake and its shores' (I. 1045). Finally, towards the end of the *Confessions* he returns again to this theme: 'J'ai toujours aimé l'eau passionnément, et sa vue me jette dans une rêverie délicieuse, quoique souvent sans objet déterminé. Je ne manquais point à mon lever lorsqu'il faisait beau de courir sur la terrasse humer l'air salubre et frais du matin, et planer des yeux sur l'horizon de ce beau lac, dont les rives et les montagnes qui le bordent enchantaient ma vue' (I. 642).

As this last statement shows, the contemplation of water is not simply a means of securing vague emotional comfort, but also forms part of the 'dawn' theme already examined. In other words, Rousseau once again gives indirect evidence of his concern with purity and innocence. No doubt the theme of water, as Bachelard shows in his book on the subject,[1] can be associated with a variety of human attitudes and modified in accordance with the demands of the individual imagination, but Rousseau's dream of a paradisaic existence reveals a consistent predilection for clear, translucent water, the water of purity and innocence. The island-paradise of Saint-Pierre is in the midst of 'a vast stretch of clear, crystalline water'. Through Julie's 'Elysium' flows 'clear, limpid water' made 'more brilliant' by the bed of 'pure, speckled gravel'. The maternal presence not only comforts, but also purifies.

As is apparent in the passages quoted from the *Confessions*, a cloudless sky can have the same purifying effect, whilst the exhilarating freshness of the air is also included as a feature of the ideal landscape. It will be recalled that the famous description of the Alps in *La Nouvelle Héloïse* contains similar physical and emotional characteristics. On the mountain-top 'the air is pure and subtle', so that it not only 'makes colours more vivid and features more

[1] Cf. G. Bachelard, *L'Eau et les rêves* (Paris, 1942).

distinct', but gives 'lightness to the body and serenity to the soul'. In these 'ethereal regions' (which this time are located in the real world and not merely in Rousseau's idealizing imagination) the observer is struck by 'the unalterable purity of the air' which rapidly communicates itself to his own soul. 'As one approaches the ethereal regions, the soul acquires something of their unchanging purity' (II. 78). In this 'new world' there is no torment or anxiety because everything suggests the peace and permanence of true paradise.

Although the predominance of the maternal side of nature may at first suggest the pervasive presence of a reality into which the self is passively absorbed, this does not in fact happen in Rousseau's case. In spite of its great influence upon him, physical nature forms only part of his paradise, an essential part no doubt, but its background rather than its primary characteristic. His consciousness of selfhood is too strong for him to allow his personality to become lost in some physical element, however primordial. Assuredly, he speaks at times of plunging 'headlong' into the 'ocean' of nature and of identifying himself with the essence of the 'universal system' but these are exceptional experiences which form part of a much wider pattern of reactions. Even the 'mother' theme is ultimately used, as we shall see, to secure an enhanced sense of selfhood; if the 'common mother' protects him from the attacks of men, she also provides him with physical conditions suitable for the attainment of a fuller personal existence. In short, the expansive aspect of Rousseau's personality is inseparable from a profound need to intensify the reality of his own being.

Far from wanting to lose his identity in the presence of the physical world, Rousseau, in moments of exhilaration, will sometimes feel himself 'the master of the whole of nature'. Already the insular ideal, with its emphasis upon Robinson Crusoe, reveals the need to be in control of nature and not its mere servant, for Crusoe himself survived by dominating his environment and imposing his will upon it. Rousseau also sees himself in the role of a discoverer and this 'exploratory' attitude leads him to compare himself to Christopher Columbus as well as Robinson Crusoe; whereas the shipwrecked Crusoe discovered his island by accident, Columbus deliberately set out on a voyage of exploration. At certain times too Rousseau has to feel that he is the true discoverer of a particular terrain, the first human being ever to set foot in it. In the course of his description of a botanizing expedition in the seventh Promenade he says: 'Et je me mis à rêver plus à mon aise en pensant que j'étais là dans un refuge ignoré de tout l'univers où les persécuteurs ne me déterreraient pas. Un mouvement d'orgueil se mêla bientôt à cette rêverie. Je me comparais à ces grands voyageurs qui découvrent une île déserte, et je me disais avec complaisance: *sans doute je suis le premier mortel qui ait pénétré jusqu'ici*; je me regardais presque comme un autre Colomb' (I. 1071). Already in the third letter to Malesherbes he had made use of a similar comparison. After greeting a day over which he had complete control with the words: 'Me voilà maître de moi pour le reste de ce jour!' he added: 'J'allais alors d'un pas plus tranquille chercher quelque lieu sauvage dans la forêt, quelque lieu désert où rien ne montrant la main des hommes n'annoncât la servitude et la domination, quelque asile où *je pusse croire avoir pénétré le premier* et où nul tiers importun ne vint s'interposer entre la nature et moi' (I. 1139–40). Saint-Preux's first reaction to the sight of Julie's 'Elysium' is in a similar vein: 'Il me semblait d'être *le premier mortel qui jamais eût pénétré dans ce désert*' (II. 471). Occasionally, as Marcel Raymond aptly puts it, Rousseau approaches this virgin territory in 'nuptial' mood as he 'tramples underfoot' the astonishing profusion of plants and flowers, excited by the feeling of his own power and vitality.

It is also worth recalling that Rousseau sometimes expressed this self-assertive, almost aggressive mood in more sombre, awesome surroundings. Equal to his aversion for flat country was his love of 'torrents, crags, fir-trees, dark woods, mountains, rough roads, and frightening precipices'. Apart from the famous mountain scenes in *La Nouvelle Héloïse*,[1] there are some interesting examples in Rousseau's personal writings. On one occasion he describes his delight in the dizziness he felt as, flat on his face, he leant over a high parapet in order to contemplate for 'hours on end' the 'blue water' far below and listen to its roaring amid the cries of the birds of prey' (I. 172).[2] In the *Rêveries* too he relates

[1] Cf. esp. Part I, Lettres XXIII & XXVI. Saint-Preux's mood is at times the exact opposite of the idyllic feelings evoked by more pleasant sights. 'Je trouve partout dans les objets la même horreur qui règne au dedans de moi' (II. 90).

[2] There are some interesting comments on this point in the article of B. Munteano already quoted, where the feeling of giddiness is associated with Rousseau's reactions to nothingness and death.

how on one of his lonely botanizing expeditions he made his way to a forbidding mountainous region enclosed by an almost impenetrable barrier of dark fir-trees and huge beeches. On this occasion too he lay 'flat on his face' in order to peer into the 'horrible precipices' and listen to the cries of the wild birds (I. 1070). Admittedly, these experiences formed only one aspect of his feelings for nature, which usually took a more cheerful form, but they show that his reactions should not be limited to a single mood.

However important as a means of bringing comfort and serenity, or of producing more disturbing and ambivalent emotions, physical nature could never be the sole basis of Rousseau's mythology. As he admitted in the *Dialogues*, his love of nature was sometimes a mere 'substitute' for human affection. Had he been able to secure the love of his fellow men, he would have been tempted to give up nature for the company of human beings. Moreover, even in his moods of imaginative reverie, the presence of nature could not completely fill his mind. As he says in the third letter to Malesherbes, his imagination would not allow him to leave the beautiful scene deserted. 'Je la peuplais bientôt d'êtres selon mon cœur, et chassant bien loin l'opinion, les préjugés, toutes les passions factices, je transportais dans les asiles de la nature des hommes dignes de les habiter. Je m'en formais une société charmante dont je ne me sentais pas indigne' (I. 1140). The 'golden age' thus created needed the presence of imaginary human beings to bring it to life.

The sequel, however, reveals that even this ideal society is not enough to fill the 'void' within him; his heart begins to reach out towards 'another kind of enjoyment', of which he feels an incomprehensible but overwhelming need; his thoughts rise from the 'surface of the earth' to 'all the beings of nature, the universal system of things, the incomprehensible being who encompasses everything' (I. 1141). Even then he wants to launch out into the infinite as the weight of a universe seems to overwhelm and stifle him. At last he can do no more than cry out in a 'bewildered ecstasy': 'O great Being! O great Being!' Ultimately, therefore, the terrestrial dream requires the presence of God to make it complete. The universe does not exist by itself but as God's creation, and man himself perceives—and then only confusedly— the true beauty of the universal system when he sees it as God's handiwork, that is, as a physical quality sustained by a divine power.

The ultimate effect of man's awareness of God's existence is to inspire him with an intense and perhaps ultimately inconceivable desire to fulfil himself as a spiritual being. Accordingly, Rousseau does not seek to lose himself in a merely passive manner. To the symbolism of 'water' should be added that of 'fire', for it is fire, rather than water, which expresses the burning enthusiasm of perfect love. No doubt the frequent use of the fire-symbol in the first part of *La Nouvelle Héloïse* owes much to the ancient tradition by which lovers use the language of hyperbole to express the overwhelming force of their emotions. Moreover, passion at the ordinary human level may seem merely to 'devour' the self and consume it in the intense ecstasy of bodily desire; but in exceptional beings like Julie and Saint-Preux the 'fire' of earthly passion can be transformed into the 'eternal flame' and 'pure, sacred fire' of 'divine' love. Human feelings thus become suffused with the mystical glow of a 'celestial fire' which purifies the soul and makes it worthy to enjoy the 'supreme felicity' of paradise.

2. *The Gods*

However self-sufficient the individual may feel in his most sublime moments, Rousseau believes that he is ultimately forced to acknowledge his dependence on his Creator; he does not exist for himself, but for God. Moreover, even in the earthly paradise of his imagination Rousseau finds support and strength in the presence of a universal system that is not just a physical entity but an expression of the divine will. Perhaps man's greatest satisfaction in this earthly life is to feel himself a part of the universal order.[1] Although paradise appears at times to be a self-contained island surrounded by a beautiful and friendly natural element, its real perfection is based on the existence of God, and its inhabitants find permanent bliss in the knowledge that they too exist in His sight. It is true that man's heart, reason, and conscience can already provide him with convincing proofs of God's existence as supreme intelligence and will, but these attributes remain impersonal and abstract until they become part of a living attitude. Rousseau feels that personal fulfilment is possible only through the presence of a

[1] Cf., *supra*, pp. 48, 94.

divine being whose gaze confers reality upon the living individual; man is never sure of the value of his being until he feels it penetrated by the divine look. Only God's presence can give permanence to the self by guaranteeing its purity and innocence; the soul that is penetrated by God's look is assured of its spiritual worth. In Rousseau's imagination, therefore, God often assumes the form of an all-seeing eye that can 'read into the depth of the heart'. Consciousness of the divine gaze assures the innocent and pure being of its reality and value. Saint-Preux tells his friend Bomston how Julie overcame possible weakness by invoking the presence of 'the righteous and redoubtable judge who sees our secret actions and can read into the depth of our hearts'. 'She was surrounded by the divine majesty; I constantly saw God between her and me!' (II. 593). Likewise, after the 'happy revolution' and 'rebirth' of her being during the wedding-ceremony, she found 'a new state' which was to 'purify her soul'. 'The eternal eye who sees everything, I told myself, now reads into the depth of my heart' (II. 354). Rousseau himself strove constantly to let God 'see into his heart'. Significantly enough, when, in his last years, he imagined himself to be enjoying a god-like omnipotence, invisibility, and goodness, he endowed himself with one of God's most remarkable attributes—the power to 'read easily into men's hearts' (I. 1058).

God's look is necessary to ensure the stability and permanence of paradise, which would not be complete—indeed, would not exist at all—if it did not find favour in God's eyes and prove itself worthy to be the object of His gaze. In this respect it is clear that Rousseau's preoccupation with the divine 'mother', however important its role in his life and work, is not the only significant element in his religious outlook. The mother-theme corresponds, on the whole, to the immanent aspect of the divine being, that which is contained within the creation itself, the vital 'nature' which gives body and substance to the universe and its creatures. From this point of view 'nature' is divine because its goodness testifies to its spiritual origin, but it does not exist in its own right and cannot be sustained by its own finite resources. Created existence depends ultimately on its Creator, on the transcendent Being who exists for and by Himself, and yet assures the permanence and tranquillity of the world He has brought into being. God, therefore, is not only made manifest in the immediate, comforting presence of the created nature from which man's own being has sprung but also in the somewhat more distant and mysterious transcendence of the divine gaze.

However, because God is the all-seeing eye, his separation from the world means that he can never be fully comprehensible or accessible to finite beings; he is too awesome to be a familiar feature of the earthly paradise; he remains the absolute Other. Man is never allowed to forget permanently that he is the *object* of the divine gaze, that is, of a gaze that is not without severity, especially for the soul conscious of possible guilt or the temptation of evil. God's presence, therefore, in Rousseau's view, not only brings a sense of personal reality, but also helps to confer a moral value on paradisaic existence.

While acknowledging God's ultimate transcendence as the all-seeing eye, Rousseau's imagination still needs to bring the divine being closer to his own life and to see him at work in the world. It is not simply a question of perceiving God's reality through the ordered harmony of the universal system of nature, but also of finding him in certain exceptional human figures who are invested with divine attributes. Nor is this divinization of human beings restricted to Rousseau's imaginative writing, for it was also an occasional feature of his real-life experience of paradisaic bliss. In the *Confessions*, for example, he compared Madame de Warens to God: it was impossible for him to keep any secret from her because 'his heart was open before her as before God' (I. 191). More characteristically still, the paradise of his childhood was not due solely to his cousin's affectionate companionship and the simple innocence of rural surroundings, but owed a great deal to the benevolent protection of their guardians: the Lamberciers were 'like gods who read into their hearts' (I. 21).

It is especially in *La Nouvelle Héloïse* that this process of deification finds its most elaborate expression. If Julie, Wolmar, and Bomston are superior human beings, they also possess still more remarkable qualities as gods who ensure the stability and order of the paradise of Clarens. No doubt they are polyvalent figures too, embodying various aspects of Rousseau's personal, aesthetic, and philosophical intentions; the following observations are not intended to deal exhaustively with these characters, but simply to examine their role as gods on earth, that is, as significant figures in Rousseau's religious mythology.

Julie is a particularly interesting example of Rousseau's

predilection for attributing divine qualities to human beings. Psychologically, as the idealized image of the various women whom he has loved or by whom he has been attracted, she already has a perfection which surpasses the charm and beauty of any particular woman; at the same time she embodies the spiritual element which Rousseau believed to be present in all ideal love. Admittedly, Saint-Preux's ascription of 'divine' virtues to his beloved is often little more than an echo of a very old and banal romantic tradition. Expressions like 'celestial Julie' and 'divine Julie' suggest a lover's vision rather than a sober statement of fact; when he describes her as *la divine enseigne* which gives meaning and direction to his life, Saint-Preux is perhaps merely paying tribute to her exceptional human qualities, whilst his eulogy of her as a woman whose 'sublime soul' has the 'beauty' and 'purity of the angels' does not necessarily indicate any deep spiritual conviction. Even so, his love always contains a strong vein of idealism, and Julie's innocence and purity are unique enough to arouse 'inexplicable contradictions' in an aspirant who desires as a man and loves as an idealist. From the very first Saint-Preux feels himself irresistibly drawn to this exceptional girl who enshrines within herself all the perfections of the female soul.

It is not until her wedding-day that Julie's inner nature is spiritually transformed; only a 'happy revolution' within her soul fits her to become the guide of the man whom she henceforth believes she has loved with a guilty passion. However, since in her own eyes she has been 'guilty' but not 'depraved', she has never lost her fundamental innocence and goodness. From this point onwards Julie appears as 'an expansive soul' radiating a mysterious power upon all around her, making their personalities in some sense consubstantial with her own; she possesses *une force intérieure* which cannot fail to communicate itself to others. Already in the early days of their relationship Saint-Preux declares: 'C'est lui [l'amour], qui par ta seule présence communique aux autres cœurs sans qu'ils s'en aperçoivent la tendre émotion du tien' (II. 149). In an earlier letter he affirms: 'C'était Julie elle-même qui répandait son charme invincible sur tout ce qui l'environnait' (II. 115). Nobody seems able to resist the strange attraction of her personality. 'N'as-tu jamais remarqué, mon ange', writes her friend, Claire, 'à quel point tout ce qui t'approche s'attache à toi?' (II. 203). Souls like Julie have this strange power

THE GODS

to change the quality of other people's existence. Speaking of her friend's 'invincible ascendency' over others, Claire observes: 'Voilà ce qui doit arriver à toutes les âmes d'une certaine trempe; *elles transforment pour ainsi dire les autres en elles-mêmes*; elles ont une sphère d'activité dans laquelle rien ne leur résiste: on ne peut les connaître sans les vouloir imiter, et de leur sublime élévation elles attirent à elles tout ce qui les environne' (II. 204). Claire feels her personality being 'absorbed' into her friend's, so that Julie becomes the focal point and supreme value of her existence. Like God, Julie can create 'a new being' in those who love her by 'animating' their souls with the power of her own being. 'C'est que ton cœur', says Claire, 'vivifie tous ceux qui l'environnent et leur donner pour ainsi dire un nouvel être dont ils sont forcés de lui faire hommage, puisqu'ils ne l'auraient point eu sans lui' (II. 409). It is Julie who gives reality to others by a kind of mysterious emanation and diffusion of her own personality.

She also has the capacity to transform her physical environment by imbuing it with something of her own being. This is very well brought out in the description of her 'Elysium', the little corner of Clarens which she has effectively made into a peaceful sanctuary of her own.[1] Her Elysium is a kind of private paradise within the wider paradise of Clarens. It immediately suggests to Saint-Preux the paradisaic island ideal by which Jean-Jacques himself was always haunted; for it recalls the desert islands he has visited during his trip round the world. 'O Tinian! O Juan Fernandez! le bout du monde est à votre porte' (II. 471). Saint-Preux's subsequent exploration of the Elysium merely confirms his first impression that he has been brought to a 'desert island' and a 'paradise' of a very special kind. If the physical nature of the Elysium is ultimately God's handiwork, it is Julie who animates and organizes it, breathing the spirit of her personality into a domain that is unmistakably hers. Henceforth Saint-Preux cannot separate the physical elements of the Elysium from the presence of Julie's own being. At dawn (and once again we are reminded of Rousseau's preoccupation with the theme of rebirth!) he gets up

[1] On the use of the word 'Élysée' see the editor's note, II. 1614. For a detailed commentary on *La Nouvelle Héloïse* the reader is referred to the rich and penetrating introduction and notes by Bernard Guyon in the Pléiade edition. The present study is indebted to this edition on a number of points. Valuable comments are also to be found in J. Starobinski, op. cit., pp. 99 f.

to savour all the beauty and freshness of this sacred spot. 'Ce matin je me suis levé de bonne heure, et avec l'empressement d'un enfant je suis allé m'enfermer dans l'Isle déserte ... Tout ce qui va m'environner est l'ouvrage de celle qui me fut si chère. Je la contemplerai tout autour de moi. Je ne verrai rien que sa main n'ait touché; je baiserai des fleurs que ses pieds auront foulées; je respirerai avec la rosée un air qu'elle a respiré; son goût dans ses amusements me rendra présents tous ses charmes, et *je la trouverai partout comme elle est au fond de mon cœur*' (II. 486).[1]

Although the Elysium gives the impression of spontaneous profusion and combines the exotic and familiar in a way that puts 'the end of the world at their door', it is a paradise that could belong to nobody but Julie. It is a living world, its trees and fruit bearing witness to its fertility, the song of the birds and the brightness of the flowers revealing it to be both *animé* and *sensible*; it is also an unspoilt world, offering the image of primordial innocence, for it is constantly purified by limpid streams. Most important of all, it is a haven of peace as well as of beauty; in its midst man can feel no inner torment, but only the 'eternal tranquillity' of the soul that warms it with its loving presence. Anybody fortunate enough to be granted the privilege of entering this Elysium feels his inner self being pervaded by the deep calm of its guardian's soul. 'Je me disais: la paix règne au fond de son cœur comme dans l'asile qu'elle a nommé' (II. 487).

This almost infinite capacity for permeating her environment with the essence of her own being is also accompanied by a feeling of power within her own soul; Julie is conscious of being the centre of a whole universe that derives its strength and meaning from her presence. At her happiest moment she affirms: 'Je ne vois rien qui n'étende mon être, et rien qui le divise; il est dans tout ce qui m'environne, il n'en reste aucune portion loin de moi; mon imagination n'a plus rien à faire, je n'ai rien à désirer; sentir et jouir sont pour moi la même chose' (II. 689). No doubt this sense of fulfilment creates a problem for Julie too, since she is 'satiated' with happiness and life: there is nothing more for her to experience on earth and only eternity is henceforth worthy to possess her soul. Those around her, however, are not conscious of this secret *ennui*, but only of her invincible superiority.

Julie thus seems to embody the goodness and innocence which

[1] Cf., *supra*, p. 7.

are indispensable to any true paradise. She has the capacity to sanctify everything she touches, and at times emerges as God's representative on earth, a sort of female Christ-figure incarnating the innocence and purity of the divine existence. If Claire insists that Julie cannot be 'profaned' by contact with the impure Laure, it is because her 'sublime elevation' places her above sinful mortals. Even Claire herself feels unworthy to 'touch the hem of her garment', whilst Julie does not hesitate to call Saint-Preux her 'apostle' and 'penitent'. She is a 'divine model' inspiring lesser beings with the feeling that in her presence they are already enjoying paradise on earth.

If she is so superior to ordinary mortals, it is only because she embodies in a purer form the essence of their own personality; her goodness and innocence are in some way the qualities of original being. Even her worshippers are conscious of a close affinity between her being and their own regenerated selves. This is clearly brought out not only in the power of emanation already described, but also in her maternal qualities: she is as it were a kind of divine mother, warm, protective, and yet purifying. She thus seems to embody in human form the maternal element already present in Rousseau's feeling for nature.[1] 'Divine' though she may be in certain ways, Julie expresses as it were the immanent principle of the creation rather than the transcendent spirit of its Creator. As such she does not possess the self-sufficiency of the Being who exists by Himself. In fact, attention has already been called to Julie's feeling of *ennui* and her consciousness of *un vide inexprimable* which can be filled only by life after death; she is disturbed by an eternal, infinite longing which cannot be satisfied by earthly existence. Even as the divine mother, therefore, her power is restricted, although her 'subjects', dazzled by her goodness and beauty, may not be aware of this limitation. However essential they may be to complete the perfection of paradise, goodness, innocence, and quasi-maternal love are not powerful enough to constitute its sole basis. Paradise has ultimately to be provided with a spiritual principle of another, though complementary, kind. At the risk of some simplification it may perhaps be affirmed that 'matter', as the created substance of the world, has to be completed by the power of the 'spirit'. In other words, the ideal 'mother' must ultimately acknowledge her dependence on the heavenly 'father'.

[1] Cf., *supra*, p. 102.

Moreover, Julie herself not only confesses her need for God himself, but also admits the importance of that wise guide and mentor, M. de Wolmar, who in certain ways serves as God's representative on earth. If, therefore, Julie is the symbol of the immanent divine mother, Wolmar is that of the transcendent divine father.

For the purpose of the present discussion it is proposed to ignore Wolmar the atheist—a purely extraneous and accidental character introduced into the work at a late stage for propaganda purposes. On the other hand, Wolmar the god plays an important part in the religious mythology of the novel. For Saint-Preux at least his divine quality is not in doubt. 'O mon Bienfaiteur! O mon Père! En me donnant à vous tout entier, je ne puis vous offrir, *comme à Dieu même*, que les dons que je tiens de vous' (II. 611). Wolmar's transcendent quality is also hinted at on his very first appearance. Whereas Julie is an affectionate, immediate presence, Wolmar remains throughout a rather remote and impersonal figure. Not only is he much older than the others (he calls Saint-Preux and Julie his children), but he comes from a far-off country and has a somewhat obscure past. He is primarily an *observer*, as he himself recognizes, and therefore stands aloof from other people in a kind of permanent detachment. From the very first Saint-Preux is struck by his unchanging character. 'Tel il m'a paru le premier jour, tel il me paraît le dernier sans aucune altération' (II. 372). In this respect he seems to reflect something of God's eternal self-sufficiency.

As an observer, however, he is not a merely passive figure, in spite of appearances, for if he remains apart from others, he is interested in them and *watches* them, so that they can rarely forget his penetrating gaze. This is perhaps Wolmar's most divine characteristic, for it at once recalls the gaze which Rousseau attributed to God himself. Wolmar admits that he would like to become 'a living eye', since he 'loves to read into men's hearts' (II. 491). Moreover, his piercing look is clearly that of no ordinary person: he has 'some supernatural gift for reading into the depth of people's hearts' (II. 496). This 'righteous and severe' being has 'a perspicacious eye' that misses nothing. Whenever he feels himself weakening, Saint-Preux is brought back to virtue by the thought of Wolmar's disapproving look. 'Je croyais voir son œil pénétrant et judicieux percer au fond de mon cœur et m'en faire rougir encore' (II. 487). He fears nothing so much as 'generous

Wolmar's contemptuous look'. Perhaps Saint-Preux's greatest moment of triumphant fulfilment is when he feels himself worthy to be *seen* by Womar. At the height of *la fête des vendanges*, with its atmosphere of universal joy, he exclaims: 'Je ne crains point que son œil éclairé lise au fond de mon cœur' (II. 609). Even the servants of Clarens, conscious of their master's gaze, feel impelled to show themselves as they really are.

The perspicacity of Wolmar's look offers a strictly moral challenge which, in Saint-Preux's words, 'lifts' other people 'above themselves', thereby inspiring them to achieve a 'virtue' which, as the consequence of personal effort, transcends in value the spontaneous 'goodness' of the natural man. Through this divine mentor Saint-Preux is given a 'new elevation', which allows him to be 'what he is' and 'ought to be'. As God's representative on earth, the aloof and yet benevolent Wolmar enables his subjects to rise above themselves to a higher moral plane of being.

Whereas Julie's fulfilment comes from an extension of her being into her environment and from a subsequent feeling of reigning over a universe which is a prolongation of her own personality, Wolmar's authority is such that he never allows others to feel that they are his equals. His happiness comes from the exercise of a paternal authority that rejoices in the feeling of its own god-like power. 'Seul entre tous les mortels [un père de famille] est maître de sa propre félicité, parce qu'il est heureux comme Dieu même, sans rien désirer de plus que ce dont il jouit' (II. 467).

Yet Wolmar is not content simply to exist in solitary self-sufficiency, since he rules over a domain which he makes his own through 'the most perfect relations and the most efficient control'. In short, he incarnates one of God's most remarkable powers—the creation of order. When it has once been brought into being, the world, with its material essence and intrinsic goodness, has an independent existence of its own, but in some sense it is still God's being which determines its form and structure. If Julie's personality gives a heart and soul to the paradise of Clarens, Wolmar guarantees its order and harmony. The world of human relations is the result of his organizing genius, although Julie suffuses it with the warmth of love. 'Every well-ordered house reflects the master's soul'. However, this 'sacred' authority is not arbitrary, for the very reason that a truly 'paternal house' is one in which all its members belong to the same family and strive for a common end.

Thanks to Wolmar's wisdom each person finds his place in this ordered world which seems to contain 'all the charms of the golden age'.[1] Because all accept the same authority and are united by a single purpose, they live in mutual trust and confidence. If Julie provides the goodness which animates all the inhabitants, Wolmar ensures their integrity by laying down one supreme moral principle, which, he avers, sums up all the rest: 'Ne fais ni ne dis jamais rien que tu ne veuilles que tout le monde voie et entende' (II. 424). To become a worthy inhabitant of Clarens Saint-Preux has only to 'follow the example of frankness which reigns here'. Even Julie fears that her own goodness might not be enough to sustain her if it were not for Wolmar's vigilance. 'Vivez dans le tête-à-tête', he tells Julie and Saint-Preux, 'comme si j'étais présent ou devant moi comme si je n'y étais pas; voilà tout ce que je vous demande.' Wolmar dominates the whole society of Clarens like an invisible but omniscient presence. Because of him this is a house without 'vain subtleties', for its occupants are aware of the need for frankness and openness in all their doings.[2]

The two gods would obviously be incomplete without each other, and each in fact acknowledges his debt to the other. In spite of his great moral authority Wolmar admits that he too—like all the rest—is one of Julie's 'subjects'. Without Julie's 'goodness' his 'penetration' would be cold and impersonal, just as her 'goodness' needs his 'penetration' to prevent it from becoming merely vague and formless emotion. Between them, therefore, they constitute the divine centre of this earthly paradise and embody two fundamental and complementary aspects of God's being. Through their presence the inhabitants of Clarens are given the innocence, transparency, peace, beauty, and virtue that make them worthy of the 'supreme felicity' of paradise.

Yet for the privileged few who are admitted to their intimacy Julie and Wolmar are human as well as divine beings, and, what is more, true friends. Because his dearest wish is to be acknowledged as the friend and equal of these superior beings, Saint-Preux is willing to let them 'take possession' of him and put him, as their 'pupil', through a series of 'tests' which will eventually qualify him for admission to the company of the elect. He realizes that the

---

[1] Cf., *supra*, p. 89.
[2] Cf., *supra*, pp. 38 f. for Rousseau's animadversions against 'subtlety' in the philosophical field.

function of the elect is to make new beings, to re-create nature in all its freedom and equality; Saint-Preux tells his friends that he wants to be 'a new being worthy of their confidence'. In their presence he feels his soul 'awakening' and regaining its life and strength; for them he will be 'everything he ought to be'. Having fulfilled their divine function, the gods become the equals of the humans who have benefited from their attention, or, perhaps more exactly, the humans succeed in raising themselves to the level of the gods they adore. Thanks to this beneficent influence, man can feel that he has been truly reborn.

The would-be inhabitants of Clarens are helped in their striving for perfection by the presence of other superior beings. In particular, Saint-Preux is encouraged by the friendship of Lord Bomston (a superior being of another kind!) who has admitted him to his esteem and affection. From his earliest years Rousseau had always been fascinated by 'great men', those 'great, strong souls' who dominate their environment. As a child he readily identified himself with the characters of the books he read. 'I used to become the character whose life I was reading.' He was a particularly enthusiastic reader of Plutarch, and the 'ancient men' portrayed by this author left an indelible impression on his mind; he considered 'these venerable images of antiquity' as models to be admired and imitated. Later on, in a parallel between Rome and Sparta, he affirmed: 'L'âme s'élève à son tour et le courage s'enflamme en parcourant ces respectables monuments; on participe en quelque sorte aux actions héroïques de ces grands hommes, il semble que la méditation de leur grandeur nous en communique une partie' (III. 538). He judged 'Roman pride' to be a quality capable of inspiring others to equal greatness. It is not surprising, therefore, that when he became the creator of imaginary figures, he should have imbued them with the same heroic qualities. Lord Bomston is certainly an exceptional being who, like Wolmar, seems at times to possess divine attributes. He can arouse 'sublime feelings' in others because of the remarkable nature of his own. 'Son âme sublime est au-dessus de celles des hommes, et il n'est pas plus permis de résister à ses bienfaits qu'à ceux de la divinité' (II. 219). What more can Saint-Preux desire than to win the esteem and friendship of such a man? When he secures his affection, he knows that he has earned the approbation of 'les belles âmes' and 'les âmes fortes' who reign over the paradise of Clarens. The inhabitants of Clarens are, therefore, not unlike the 'initiates' who people the ideal world of the *Dialogues*, 'these inhabitants of the enchanted world' who are so superior to ordinary men.

By achieving equality with the elect souls of paradise and by earning the right to dwell with them, Saint-Preux rejoices in the thought that his own existence has acquired the same ineffable strength and innocence. These privileged beings possess *une grande force d'âme* which fills them with a divine enthusiasm that sets them above base desires. Already on his return from his trip round the world Saint-Preux is told by Bomston that he can now be confident of his own inner strength, for 'the sight of a sublime and pure soul, triumphing over its passions and ruling over itself, is the one you are now enjoying' (II. 524).

The ultimate happiness of these 'privileged souls' is to know that they are completely open to one another. Being transparent to God's gaze, it is natural that they should also become transparent to one another. In this respect the 'divine friendship' of paradise recalls the most striking characteristic of primitive men—'la facilité de se pénétrer réciproquement' (III. 8). Their innocence in the sight of God enables them to enjoy this spontaneous interpenetration of consciousness. The mutual confidence of Clarens has the same quality of pure innocence and transparence, but it has a higher spiritual value than the unreflecting innocence of primitive man, since it is based on a clear awareness of purity and openness of heart. Julie sums up the true nature of their happiness when she says: 'Convenez, du moins, que tout le charme de la société qui régnait entre nous est dans cette ouverture de cœur qui met en commun tous les sentiments, toutes les pensées, et qui fait que chacun se sentant tel qu'il doit être se montre à tous tel qu'il est' (II. 689). The enjoyment of this openness and intimacy is enhanced by the knowledge that the paradise of Clarens is an 'island' separated from the rest of the world—a completely self-enclosed community, capable of living on its own resources and for its own ends.

The perfect felicity of these exceptional beings is vividly described in the famous *matinée à l'anglaise* (*La Nouvelle Héloïse*, V. 3: II. 555–61). This is the true meeting-place of friends who, far from wanting to achieve some practical good, are content to enjoy their own and one another's being. Just as paradise is an abode of pure contemplation and peace, so is it a place for *recueillement*, inner meditation and reciprocal affection.

In the first place, these friends enjoy this openness and frankness, which we have already seen to be an essential condition of paradise as a place of light. 'Il n'est rien resté dans le fond des cœurs qu'on veuille se cacher l'un à l'autre' (II. 557). If Saint-Preux henceforth rejoices in the possession of a 'new being', it is because he now knows that he has passed Wolmar's 'tests' and can say with pride: 'At last I shall dare to show myself to him.' Transformed by a 'new elevation', he now feels that he has become what he 'wants' and 'ought to be'. Thanks to this complete intimacy and confidence, the friends of Clarens enjoy their own being and others' affection: they lead an ideal life that combines the pleasure of being together with *la douceur du recueillement*.

Such is the perfection of their experience that it not only defies description, but involves a form of contemplation that completely dispenses with the use of language as a means of communication. The *matinée à l'anglaise* requires the presence of friends who meet in silence. Being open to one another, they have no need of words to express their thoughts; they are content to enjoy the feeling of their own existence. Whereas 'easy chatter' is the mark of 'mediocre attachments', true friendship can dispense with language. 'L'amitié! sentiment vif et céleste, quels discours sont dignes de toi? Quelle langue ose être ton interprète? Jamais ce qu'on dit à son ami peut-il valoir ce qu'on sent à ses côtés?' That is why lesser beings are excluded from this select society, for the intrusion of an alien voice would destroy the quiet charm of true intimacy. As Saint-Preux puts it in a curious phrase, 'les amis ont besoin d'être sans témoin *pour pouvoir ne se rien dire*, à leur aise' (II. 558). There is a kind of interpenetration of personal being which is an end in itself and produces its own characteristic type of bliss—'cette immobilité d'extase, plus douce mille fois que le froid repos des dieux d'Epicure' (II. 558).

Whenever they feel the need to communicate with one another, these friends do not have recourse to 'the cold intermediary of the spoken word', but to gestures. 'Mon Dieu! qu'une main serrée, qu'un regard animé, qu'une étreinte contre la poitrine, que le soupir qui la suit disent de choses, et que le premier mot qu'on prononce est froid après tout cela!' (II. 558.) In this respect the inhabitants of Clarens are like the ideal beings described in the first of the *Dialogues*, who recognize one another not by any words they use but by a 'characteristic sign' understood only by the 'initiates'. This sign is unique and inimitable because its meaning depends on the heart and not on the voice; 'it is true as soon as it is felt'; gestures are permeated by the personality of the initiate in a way that always enables the true 'brother' to be distinguished from the mere counterfeit.

At last, then, in the paradisaic intimacy of Clarens, Saint-Preux has found complete fulfilment. To the turbulence of passion has succeeded true serenity and peace, and with the purification of his feelings he achieves a state of being that seems to set him apart from ordinary people. 'Les feux dont j'ai brûlé m'ont purifié; je n'ai plus rien d'un homme ordinaire' (II. 678). Henceforth he hopes to take his place in 'this abode of innocence and peace', in a house which will always be for him 'the temple of virtue'. He now possesses a new being, which transports him to the magic surroundings of a unique world, inhabited by exceptional beings who have been able to create their own felicity.

If paradise seems a curiously aristocratic place, reserved for the few select souls who have discovered the secret of the elusive but profound intimacy of *la matinée à l'anglaise*, the gods of Clarens realize that the humbler inhabitants also have the right to enjoy a happiness not vouchsafed to the world of the unregenerate. Maybe this will fall short of the supreme felicity experienced by the elect, but its originality and spontaneity will make it worthy of paradise. The particular feature of the servants' happiness is that, unlike the self-enclosed intimacy of their masters, it takes the form of a collective enjoyment shared by the whole community. To *la matinée à l'anglaise* of the masters corresponds *la fête des vendanges* of the workers.

This episode having been analysed with remarkable penetration by Jean Starobinski,[1] I propose to consider here only those aspects which are especially relevant to the delineation of Rousseau's religious mythology. The ritual-like nature of this event is due partly to its own intrinsic characteristics, and partly to the fact that it takes place under the benevolent gaze of the divine Julie and Wolmar, those 'respected masters' who help to ensure its sacred character. In any case, it is they who are the real, if unobtrusive, organizers of the *fête*. For most of the time they remain apart, protective and watchful, their participation being limited to the direction of some particularly significant moment, as when, for

[1] Op. cit., pp. 114 f.

example, at the end of the *fête* Julie hands the burning torch to the worker she adjudges worthy to light the fireworks, this true *feu de joie* which concludes the 'august ceremony'. The pervasive influence of the 'beneficent fairy' who helps to direct the 'magic operations' reveals her once again as an 'incomparable being' who cannot fail to exercise a 'despotic' influence over her 'loving people'.

Although this popular event cannot hide the superiority of the goddess of the feast, the diffusion of universal joy gives the impression of equality and freedom. This is a kind of fertility-rite inspired by the intoxicating power of the vines and their 'beneficent fruit', which brings everybody together in a common joy. Momentarily, at any rate, the artificial barriers which normally separate men from their fellows are removed and all seem to be equal sharers of the same happiness. Even though the social distinction between masters and servants is forgotten rather than abolished,[1] the deeper human unity of the event gives the impression that 'the pleasant equality which reigns here re-establishes the order of nature' (II. 608). 'Everybody is equal and nobody forgets himself.' This is possible because the spirit of simplicity is everywhere as all enjoy the activities of rural life. Moreover, this simplicity is not that of the ecstatic immobility of *la matinée à l'anglaise*, but the joyful spirit of busy people engaged in the same useful and agreeable activity. For them work and play are identical, because everything is subordinated to a common operation that brings joy and fulfilment to all its participants.

As one might expect in the paradise of Rousseau's imagination, the joyful and active simplicity of *la fête des vendanges* is also a scene of remarkable innocence. This is indeed a day spent in 'work, gaiety, and innocence', reminiscent in so many ways of those patriarchal Biblical times when 'affectionate and modest women' and 'simple, contented men' shared in the happiness and innocence of pastoral life (II. 605). Saint-Preux invokes the memory of Rachel, Ruth, and Naomi as women whose lives revealed the same qualities of beauty, simplicity, gaiety, and innocence.

There is, however, one striking difference between the servants'

[1] Cf. J. Starobinski, op. cit., pp. 120 f., for some penetrating comments on the paternalist aspect of this episode. Cf. also some interesting observations in L. G. Crocker's article, 'Julie ou la nouvelle duplicité', *Annales Jean-Jacques Rousseau*, XXXVI (1963–5), pp. 104–52.

paradise and the masters'. Whereas *la matinée à l'anglaise* was an intimate occasion remarkable above all for the supreme bliss of silent contemplation and communion, the *fête*, as we have seen, is an essentially popular event, with a happiness of a different kind: its joy expresses itself publicly in the form of music and dancing. The medium of universal joy is neither the silence of the elect nor the chatter of the vulgar, but a paean of happiness in which human song is mingled with nature's sounds. On all sides can be heard the melody of joyful hearts singing in unison—and in Rousseau's paradise melody, not harmony, is the inevitable musical form, for unison, as he cannot forbear to point out in the course of the letter, is the only adequate means of expressing nature's feelings! The harvesters' songs are based on 'simple, naïve, often sad, and yet pleasing words, reminiscent of the moving accents of ancient times'. To human voices are added the noise of the casks being bound, the 'hoarse sound of rural instruments', the tramping of busy workers taking the harvest to the press. Everything contributes to 'the pleasant and touching picture of general gladness' which seems to cover the face of the earth. The rising sun lifts the veil of early morning mist to reveal a 'charming sight' inspired by a truly 'festive air' and heralding a day that is to be spent in song and laughter. As evening approaches and the workers relax with singing and dancing, Saint-Preux feels deeply moved by the unity, simplicity, innocence, peace, and joy of the scene. Indeed, so complete is the day that he would like to see it go on for ever, for it is 'a day spent in work, gaiety, innocence, and one would not be sorry to begin again on the morrow, the day after that, and the whole of one's life' (II. 611).

This world is both popular and sacred, because its joy and innocence not only express the goodness of nature, but also take place before the approving gaze of the gods themselves. It recalls the simplicity of early times when primitive men liked to have the gods as 'witnesses of their actions'; only with the establishment of the first societies and the advent of organized religion did they grow tired of these 'inconvenient spectators', whom they then banished into 'magnificent temples'. With *la fête des vendanges* human beings recover the sense of their own reality, as they work and sing beneath the sunny sky and once more feel blessed by the benevolent protection of the deity. In this respect the *fête* recalls the ideal public festival described by Rousseau in the *Lettre à d'Alembert*, when he imagines his fellow Genevans, like the Greeks of old, enjoying 'this great and splendid entertainment, given beneath the sky, before a whole nation'. 'It is in the open air,' he tells them, 'it is beneath the sky that you must come together and give yourselves up to the sweet feeling of your happiness.' In the paradise of Clarens this experience is still more wonderful because its inhabitants, having lost all the constraints and anxieties of civilized life, feel themselves to be completely fulfilled in the presence of God and nature.

3. Hell

Theologically Rousseau has no firm doctrine of hell. He believes that the after-life of the wicked is completely beyond the understanding of the good, who cannot envisage a mode of existence so completely at variance with their own. Whereas the good are granted some insight into the nature of their future bliss by the enjoyment of certain privileged experiences that seem to foreshadow the perfection of the world to come, it is difficult for them to imagine the condition of those who deliberately seek to violate the divine order by making it subservient to their own selfish desires. In any case, it is useless and unnecessary for the good to try to determine the fate of the wicked, since all speculation on such a matter is bound to be inconclusive. How, for example, is the idea of eternal punishment to be reconciled with the notion of God's infinite goodness? Only a 'vain curiosity', insists Rousseau, would attempt to answer such a question. All the good man needs to believe is that there will be no evil in paradise. Whether the souls of the wicked are annihilated at death or whether God's clemency makes ultimate salvation possible he does not know. Assuredly, he would expect his own happiness to be increased, rather than diminished, by the thought that his wicked 'brother' had at last been redeemed, but this is an issue which only God himself can resolve in the fullness of time.

If the idea of hell plays little part in Rousseau's religious thought, it is also absent from the earthly paradise of his imagination. He was always proud to have written a novel without villains or real wickedness. Although the noble characters of *La Nouvelle Héloïse* inevitably lack the complete perfection of the inhabitants of the celestial paradise, their short-comings are those of frailty rather than of wickedness: the imperfections of the paradise of Clarens are the result of weakness and insufficiency, not of evil intent. Very revealing in this respect is the character of the inhabitants of the ideal world described in the *Dialogues*. If they are not perfect in any divine sense, they never lose their essential goodness and innocence, because they always follow their natural impulses. 'All the first movements of nature are good and right' (I. 668). They fall short of perfection through a kind of inertia or lack of energy which allows good intentions to be frustrated by external obstacles; it is a 'weakness of soul' that in no way alters the 'original character' of their 'primitive passions'. Their whole aspiration towards *l'état céleste* has a positive motive, a desire for enjoyment which leaves no room for evil thoughts and feelings; unlike wicked men, they do not wish to possess but to *be*. Having escaped from the disastrous effects of socially conditioned *amour-propre*, they are content to savour their own *amour de soi* in all its plenitude.

A still more compelling reason for the exclusion of evil from Rousseau's dream world is his strong personal aversion to unpleasant ideas. He himself speaks of 'this reluctance to harbour gloomy, disagreeable thoughts' (I. 852). 'Cette même imagination si riche en tableaux riants et remplis de charmes rejette obstinément les objets de douleur et de peine, ou du moins elle ne les lui peint jamais si vivement que sa volonté ne les puisse effacer . . . [Jean-Jacques] se refuse aux souvenirs tristes et déplaisants qui sont inutiles, pour livrer son cœur tout entier à ceux qui le flattent' (I. 858). His conscious mind, therefore, considers wickedness to be incompatible with his true character.

In spite of the absence of evil from the 'empyrean' in which his imagination likes to dwell, Rousseau acknowledges the melancholy truth that in this world, at least, evil does find a place. 'Man' may indeed be good, but 'men' are wicked. 'I see evil on the earth', admits the Vicaire sadly. The existence of wickedness is an inescapable fact, and the human scene is one of 'disorder', 'confusion' and 'chaos'. Even though Rousseau believes his own heart to be untainted by any inclination to evil, he knows that he has been guilty of wrong-doing; he admits that the impulse to write his *Confessions* is partly due to the need to alleviate the burden of past guilt. He admits that his goodness and innocence have to some extent been corrupted by the pernicious influence of society, which has alienated him from his true self and made him act against his own nature and principles. 'False shame' and shyness have inhibited the spontaneous expression of his natural feelings and caused him to contradict his own professed ideals.

Although evil, as has already been pointed out in our examination of Rousseau's ideas, is extraneous to man's original nature, the unfortunate result of a disastrous historical accident, it still remains a fact that has to be faced. Even if Rousseau is able to exclude the idea of sin from the paradise of *La Nouvelle Héloïse*, a nagging sense of his own guilt and the apparent evidence of wickedness in others compel him to allow some place to evil in his personal world. Briefly, he solves the problem in a way that seems to accord with his philosophical outlook by a persistent and uncompromising determination to project evil outwards; forced to acknowledge its reality, he locates it in a world outside himself and the essential nature of man. The very idea of paradise as a self-contained abode presupposes the need to banish all those dark and sinister forces that threaten to disturb the peace and innocence of its happy inhabitants. However, Rousseau knows that he is incapable of losing himself indefinitely in the exaltation of his 'sublime contemplations', and that his personal paradise has to reckon at some point with the existence of evil in the world.

Since his earthly paradise depends largely on the activity of his imagination, the still wider universe of which it forms part necessarily reflects some of the contradictions of the imaginative process. If his imagination allows him to soar aloft in the empyrean of perfect contemplation, it also torments him from time to time with fear and anxiety. He is inclined to carry everything to extremes, whether for good or for ill. More especially, the sensations upon which his imagination operates often produce an unstable world of ambiguous 'signs'. Refusing to admit any absolute sinfulness within his own nature, Rousseau none the less sees himself constantly threatened by powerful forces, which, though outside himself, appear always to affect him in some strangely disturbing manner. The sinister aspect of these forces is revealed through signs and images he believes to be mysteriously controlled by evil men bent on his destruction. This is interestingly brought out in his reactions to the portrait of him painted by the famous Scottish artist, Allan Ramsay. 'This terrible portrait' is described in the *Dialogues* as that of a 'frightful

Cyclop'; Rousseau obstinately refuses to accept as his own the element of brooding introspection and anxiety which the artist has brilliantly evoked in his picture. He therefore rejects the portrait as a sinister and deliberate attempt on the part of his enemies to ridicule and degrade him in the eyes of contemporaries. Wicked men have deliberately fabricated a false 'Jean-Jacques' whom they want to pass off as the real man!

If paradise is remarkable for its light and transparence, hell, as we might imagine, becomes associated in Rousseau's imagination with the notion of darkness and mystery. 'L'innocente joie aime à s'évaporer au grand jour, mais le vice est ami des ténèbres, et jamais l'innocence et le mystère n'habitèrent longtemps ensemble' (II. 457). Wicked men work constantly in subterranean darkness like 'moles'. In his later writings especially, Rousseau sees the world divided between the forces of good and evil. Admittedly, he does not interpret the situation in any Manichaean sense, since only goodness, not evil, is an original quality of existence; evil is in some sense adventitious, and for that very reason obscure, being inconsistent with the essence of the creation. Even so, the seeming triumph of evil on this earth makes the workings of Providence difficult to understand and presents the good and innocent man with a desperate and frightening situation. However confident he may be about the ultimate vindication of divine justice, Rousseau cannot help feeling that his own suffering on this earth is an example of monstrous iniquity. Why should there be a universal plot to oppress a single good man like himself? Goodness is seen as a rapidly contracting circle of light, with himself standing isolated at its centre and threatened on all sides by the advancing forces of darkness. At such times it is often impossible for him to distinguish between the cruel decrees of an implacable 'destiny' and the beneficent activities of a divine 'Providence'; both seem to reveal themselves in the same ambiguous manner.

He finds it difficult to believe that men have deliberately, and of their own accord, invented the idea of the universal plot. Evil is like an epidemic that spreads rapidly without its victims' being aware of its exact source or their own vulnerability. In the darkness of the evil world, therefore, a curious reversal of roles takes place: whereas in heaven the elect provide the model and inspiration of all would-be seekers of felicity, in hell the wicked become the instigators of attacks upon the good. In the *Dialogues* Rousseau sees 'these gentlemen' as responsible for 'initiating' their 'little pupils' into the 'secrets of the sect', thus making them 'emissaries and operators of veiled iniquities' (I. 966). In this way wicked men extend their 'cruel influence' around them, and, securing the obedience of their disciples by the evil they induce them to commit, they form 'an indissoluble body from which each member can no longer be separated'. It is, therefore, necessary to distinguish, on the one hand, between 'the authors of the plot', its 'directors of both sexes', and 'the small number of their confidants initiated perhaps into the secret of the imposture', and, on the other, the ignorant public, which is merely deceived into lending its support to the perpetration of falsehood and calumny.

If, therefore, paradise becomes an increasingly attractive refuge for the unhappy Jean-Jacques, he finally believes that only its celestial form will be capable of offering him permanent protection against the power of evil. The world itself seems to be a truly demonic place. His enemies, he is sure, want to 'bury him alive in a coffin', or else 'ensnare' him inextricably in the 'nets' of their wicked plots. The familiar features of the world are being gradually obliterated by an 'impenetrable veil' of darkness. As soon as evil men have destroyed the innocent Jean-Jacques, they will no doubt turn their fury upon one another. Then indeed will it become clear that the earth has been transformed into a veritable hell. 'La terre devenue un enfer ne serait couverte que de Démons occupés à se tourmenter les uns les autres' (I. 954). Meanwhile, the innocent Jean-Jacques sees himself as the last defender of goodness in a world where 'devilish' beings make him the object of their 'hellish ruses'; he is the constant target of 'their burning hatred, as immortal as the Demon inspiring it' (I. 998). All familiar landmarks having disappeared, he remains confronted by 'an incomprehensible chaos in which he perceives nothing at all' (I. 995). Plunged into 'horrible darkness', he has the feeling of living on a 'strange planet' and of being the helpless victim of 'the most iniquitous and absurd system which an infernal mind could invent' (I. 1077).

The only means of living with this nightmarish existence is to look upon his destiny as a 'pure fatality' completely removed from the rational domain of cause and effect. With the spread of evil individual men lose their separate identity and, suddenly bereft of all human characteristics, are changed into impersonal forces, 'mechanical beings' whose behaviour is to be explained solely through physical 'impulse' and the 'laws of motion'; they are 'differently moved masses', devoid of all morality, and little more than robots obeying some external power beyond their control.

Yet, however impersonal and inhuman evil may seem to be to unhappy sufferers in this world, Rousseau knows that wickedness is usually communicated through the agency of his fellow men, who in some mysterious manner are able to transform the nature of the very phenomenon by which he actually seeks salvation—the look. As we have seen, the inhabitants of paradise enjoy the perfection of their own being because they feel it to be open to the approval of God's gaze; in the same way the happiness of Clarens depends on the benevolent and watchful presence of the god-like Julie and Wolmar. Yet even there the divine look is not without its awesome aspect, for it warns as well as exhorts, although its essential purpose is to encourage man to good rather than to deter him from evil. Likewise, Wolmar is 'stern' as well as 'righteous' and Saint-Preux is never allowed completely to forget the terrible consequences of any deviation from rectitude, but, here again, the main function of the divine look is to provide assurance and security. If, as a means of moral regeneration, it makes a challenging impact upon the individual by reminding him of the implications of failure, it also provides him with positive means of achieving success. In heaven, of course, victory over evil will have been definitely won, but in an earthly paradise happiness remains precarious and is never certain of having escaped the threat of failure. In the plenitude of felicity there is somewhere concealed the tiny crack through which evil may steal unexpectedly upon the unwary. However, this remains only a vague possibility against which the innocent and good man can easily secure protection by resolutely opening himself to the beneficent influence of the divine countenance. In the everyday world, on the other hand, the situation is made much more dangerous by the manifest and inescapable presence of wicked men. However confident he may be in the strength of his own virtue, the innocent man will always know himself to be the object of the hostile gaze of evil-doers. If the divine gaze can lift a man above himself, endow him with a new being and make him a new man, the gaze of the wicked can alienate the good but weak man from his true nature and invest him with an artificial self that others may accept as the real person. In this way he is reduced to the status of a mere object, which the world either mistakenly or deliberately claims to be the true man.

In his last years Rousseau found it almost impossible to forget 'the anxious and vigilant eye which they incessantly fastened upon him' (I. 951); he was, he believed, the permanent object of 'malevolent' and 'mocking' looks, and even when he sought refuge amid the solitude of nature and was able to forget for a short time his tormenters' evil gaze, he was convinced they would never forget *him*. Hell on earth was to be located in the sinister look of wicked men.

Nevertheless, hell, by its very nature, is not a permanent part of Rousseau's religious mythology, since it has no power to affect the happiness of those who succeed in entering paradise. Evil may continue to stalk the earth, but the good man, safe in the heavenly refuge, will have no cause to fear it any longer. His whole being will henceforth be filled with the light of the divine gaze and darkness will be banished for ever. The elect will be able to enjoy the contemplation of a personal existence permeated by innocence, light, peace, and beauty. By identifying themselves with their own being the inhabitants of paradise will also be attuned to the goodness of the divine order; every perfected human soul will rejoice in the awareness of his own existence, because he knows that it forms part of God's creation. Already on this earth the good man obtains brief glimpses of the bliss to come as he feels his life attuned to the harmony of the universal system. In moments of unhappiness, too, he can find comfort in the reassuring presence of 'mother-nature', whilst in moments of doubt or uncertainty he feels himself lifted up by the gaze of the heavenly father. At peace with the creation and its Creator, he will at last be able to enjoy in untroubled tranquillity the delights of the heavenly paradise, that self-sufficient island of bliss in which the good find their true reward.

CONCLUSION

ONE of Rousseau's principal aims was to restore to a corrupt civilization some of the innocence and goodness with which God had originally endowed his creation. Without these qualities, he believed, man could never be happy because he could never be himself. True fulfilment involved the plenitude of a personal existence freed from inner division and external obstacle; whereas the life of modern man was based for the most part on 'opinion' and 'appearance', a regenerated existence would owe everything to 'nature' and 'reality'. Yet, according to Rousseau, in a world dominated by subtlety and sophistication the apparently simple lessons of nature were the most difficult to learn, for man had been diverted from his proper goal by a long historical process which concealed his true being beneath an artificial mask of false values. Since most contemporaries accepted this mask as the real self, it was necessary first of all to point out the exact nature of their error before presenting them with a portrait of man's true features.

Religion had inevitably shared the deterioration of all other human values, but since it was the ultimate basis of any valid human outlook, its decadence had had a particularly disastrous effect upon the search for happiness. In the first place, religion had been gravely debilitated by a process of constant reflection, which destroyed 'the soul's vigour'; an increasing subtlety of dogma had been accompanied by a corresponding decline in moral strength. In the second place, whenever it avoided this evil, religion suffered still more serious corruption at the hands of those who made it the instrument of intense but dangerous passions, which generated bigotry and intolerance instead of love and charity. In any case, human judgement had been so perverted and the whole hierarchy of human values so completely disrupted that a very difficult task faced anybody who wanted to recover the sense of his own reality and understand the proper place of religion in human existence.

Because of the gravity of the situation Rousseau proposed that men should begin their quest anew by going back to the very foundations of religion. Personal fulfilment required the rediscovery of principles which were certain and immediate in their appeal and possessed the unity and simplicity of essential truth. This meant that the clarification of man's authentic nature and the elucidation of the basis of natural religion were simply two complementary aspects of the same essential process, because all authentic existence was ultimately based on spiritual truth. Nevertheless, since it was a question of rediscovering the sources of human nature and of finding certain simple but fundamental facts about man's existence and the still wider reality of which it formed part, any thinker who undertook this task in a corrupt world had to do much more than make a merely intellectual re-appraisal of the situation; sound thinking presupposed a personal regeneration and renewal of experience that could be achieved only through an active effort of will and an overwhelming determination to resist all those insidious influences that prevented man from reaching the truth. It was not enough to expose the falsity of contemporary values, however important this task might be; it was also necessary to provide the means of renewing the living experience upon which all sound thinking had ultimately to be based.

At this point Rousseau was confronted by a difficulty: where, in a corrupt age, was that primordial, original experience to be found? Certainly not among contemporary leaders and philosophers whose life and work merely reflected current 'opinion'; the great men of the past were perhaps worthier of imitation, but, in their case, it was often difficult for a modern man to recover a true likeness, because all historical reconstruction depended on the often misleading and unreliable testimony of the written word. Moreover, historical example was ineffectual without the active co-operation of the present experience that alone could give it real meaning. Ultimately, therefore, Rousseau felt obliged to begin with the only experience he could accept as reliable—his own. As is apparent from his own account of his religious quest, he realized that even the sincerest man's examination of his experience was fraught with difficulty, for it was constantly exposed to the insidious influence of society and personal feelings (such as fear and shame), which prevented the achievement of complete honesty. In spite of these obstacles Rousseau believed that it was solely through 'withdrawing into himself' and 'consulting his own heart' that a man could ever hope to find out the truth about himself and the human situation; ultimately his existence could be based only on those truths he had made truly his own.

Because the advocate of sincerity was obliged to look beyond the superficial world of appearances, he knew that the most important truths—those of religion—were not to be found in the merely empirical aspects of everyday life. Although it was never a question of ignoring the reality of immediate experience and of seeking refuge in some superterrestrial world of Platonic perfection, it was still essential to see human existence in the light of its ideal possibilities. Immediate experience had to be deepened and enriched in a way that allowed its spiritual significance to emerge in the circumstances of ordinary life. The real and the ideal were not to be separated, but interpreted in terms of each other. No doubt that was why Rousseau's *Confessions* were intended to deal with the events of his life in a special way; they portrayed a man involved in a truly human situation, and yet their ultimate emphasis was not upon the incidents themselves, however picturesque or dramatic they might sometimes seem to be, but upon the 'history of his most secret feelings' and the 'secret history of his soul'; it was this 'ideal' aspect of himself, this 'inner model', which Rousseau hoped would serve as a mirror to other men by enabling them to perceive in it something of their own original being.

When the author of the *Confessions* wrote 'Let every reader imitate me and withdraw into himself, as I have done', he was undoubtedly thinking of the effect of his subsequent self-examination upon other people's estimate of his character, but he was also stressing a principle that played an important part in his didactic writings. Any sincere teacher had to begin by recounting to his would-be pupil the history of his own search for truth, for this was the first and obvious guarantee of his honesty and seriousness of purpose. It was natural for the Vicaire savoyard to start his 'profession of faith' with a kind of confession, relating 'in the simplicity of his heart' the story of his failures and triumphs; only then did he feel justified in asking his young friend to consult his own inner being. Assuredly, Rousseau acknowledged that every individual's life was unique and exceptional in many ways, but the narration of his personal experience was intended to serve as an incentive to other men to undertake the same prolonged and earnest self-examination; they would then find that in some strange but inevitable way their own particular lives formed part of the history of man himself. Sincerity presupposed this important truth: the individual could win through to the universal as soon as he realized that the meaning and essence of his own personality was bound up with the nature and destiny of his fellow men.

The discovery of the individual's ideal possibilities would thus enable him to bridge the gap between his limited personal experience and the wider realm of universal human nature; as soon as he had found his true nature, he would no longer feel imprisoned within his own subjective world, for he had been given access to values valid for all men of good faith. In this sense Rousseau may be said to belong to the old metaphysical tradition, inasmuch as he believed that the meaning of man's life was inseparable from that of reality as a whole, but he substituted a personal starting-point for the intellectual, rational approach of early thinkers;[1] the link between the individual and the objective world was not established primarily through intellectual speculation, but through the active participation of his whole being in the reality that was of 'interest' to him and that it was 'important for him to know'. This did not mean, in Rousseau's opinion, that a man's investigation of his situation had to be restricted, even at the philosophical level, to merely pragmatic and utilitarian issues, but that he had first of all to concentrate on those principles which were of immediate and vital concern to his existence as a complete human being. To find these fundamental truths he had to use the resources of his whole nature, and not some limited part of it. Reason, heart, conscience, all had their part to play in the establishment of a valid philosophy of life; the loss of any of these original features of human existence inevitably meant its impoverishment and mutilation. As we have seen, Rousseau did not attack reason as such, but only the mere 'reasoning' which went no further than superficial subtleties. Certain truths—for example, the true nature of God or the soul—might well lie beyond the range of reason, but they could never be against it. If Rousseau at times appeared to diminish reason's role, it was largely because of his mistrust of the false 'reflection' of contemporary philosophers. Likewise, he insisted that feeling could be a source of error whenever it took the form of selfish pride or passion and failed to recognize the rights of essential human

---

[1] Cf. P. Burgelin, *La Philosophie de l'existence de J.-J. Rousseau*, pp. 567 ff., for an important discussion of this point.

capacities. Both reason and feeling had to acknowledge their dependence upon conscience and will. If man needed reason to 'know' the good, it was conscience alone that enabled him to 'love' it and freedom that allowed him to 'choose' it.

According to Rousseau, then, a valid religious outlook was impossible without some kind of philosophical system. In his last years he insisted upon the essential unity of his own 'interconnected system' of 'deeply thought things'. If he shared contemporary hostility to abstract metaphysical systems, it was mainly because he considered them to be without adequate roots in reality and experience. When seen in its true light, *amour de soi*, unlike selfish *amour-propre*, enabled man to take his place in a wider realm of being, for it was an 'original' quality of human existence and inseparable from the principle of order. Man could not rediscover the true meaning of his experience until he had understood his proper place in the universal system, whilst his comprehension of that system largely depended, in its turn, on a proper view of his own existence. As soon as he became aware of his true being, he would appreciate the profound harmony existing between his 'immortal nature' and the 'constitution of this world'; there was a close link between the moral order of human life and the spiritual order of the universe. Man was not a strange anomaly in some vast material system, but a meaningful and valuable part of a creation remarkable for its ordered harmony and beauty. Any sincere observer who followed the prompting of his whole nature could not fail, in Rousseau's view, to respond to this fundamental fact. If man obtained such a very deep satisfaction from the feeling of his own existence, it was largely because this existence formed part of a still greater order of being.

In an age of doubt and scepticism Rousseau saw himself as a thinker who offered his fellow men an optimistic view of their situation, provided that they would turn away from the false values of contemporary society and seek once again the fundamental truths on which every happy existence had finally to rest. However great the evils he saw around him, the sincere man could have confidence in the power of regeneration, for God had provided him with the strength and the natural goodness which could lead him to complete fulfilment. He needed no supernatural revelation, no elaborate ecclesiastical organization, in fact, no intermediaries of any kind, to bring him to a direct, immediate awareness of religious truth. The Church was at most an instrument of social discipline, and utterly devoid of any spiritual powers that were not accessible to all men who sincerely 'withdrew into themselves' and sought to rediscover their 'original' nature. The renewal of man's spiritual life was his own responsibility; God had given him the power and the means of finding his own salvation.

Any view of existence that denied the importance of spiritual values was, in Rousseau's eyes, extremely pessimistic, for it placed the rich and powerful of this world in a privileged position by depriving the poor of all hope of betterment in the next. Towards the end of his life he deplored 'this convenient philosophy of the happy and rich who made their paradise in this world'. Contrary to contemporary philosophical opinion, he believed that materialism discouraged efforts to achieve real happiness, since it robbed the poor and unhappy of all genuine incentive by blinding them to the spiritual and moral possibilities of their existence; it was a cruel and insidious philosophy, in that it presented an entirely false portrait of human nature. It made 'interest'—the petty, egotistical interest of the modern world, not the deeper 'interest' of the sincere seeker of the truth—man's sole guide and unbridled passions his only god (I. 971). A 'barbarous doctrine', in so far as it denied the need of virtue and justice and rejected the whole idea of the universe as the embodiment of a rational and spiritual principle, materialism ran counter to that 'moral order of which nothing here below could give an adequate idea', because it 'had its seat in a different system for which people vainly looked on this earth, but to which everything one day would be brought back' (I. 672). Any man who foolishly abandoned himself to the 'interest of this life' and the domination of his senses was repudiating his destiny as a human being; he was turning his back upon spiritual values meant to bring him closer to himself, his fellow men, and the sublime beauty of the 'universal system'.

As we have seen, Rousseau's constant affirmation of the need for sincerity led him to seek greater depth and simplicity in religious experience. In the noblest sense of the term man had to rediscover the meaning of 'naïveté'. To obtain a vivid awareness of spiritual reality he had to free himself from the sophistication and subtlety of contemporary values and re-establish direct contact with the personal source of truth; his first duty was to live out those truths that made an immediate appeal to his whole being. The attainment of man's ultimate goal—the unity and plenitude of an existence that was 'without obstacle or diversion'—would be impossible until he had learnt the lesson of simplicity, innocence, and goodness.

Rousseau acknowledged that his own striving for unity and perfection had been compelled to overcome some formidable obstacles. Indeed, his desire for self-realization was partly inspired by the need to abolish inner tension and conflict; he knew that his mind, heart, and imagination often pulled him in different directions. Even so, he was quite convinced that his salvation depended on spiritual values capable of satisfying all the essential elements of his personality, however diverse their outward expression. The longing for simple, immediate, and complete fulfilment involved all his aspirations towards the ideal, whether at the personal, philosophical, or imaginative level. Yet the very fact that it was necessary for him to reach 'man' by first of all exploring the depths of his own being was, in Rousseau's view, striking proof of the decadence of contemporary values. However disconcerting the contradictions of his own nature, he never seriously doubted his essential goodness or that of the humanity to which he belonged; he felt sure that the cause of his own inner conflicts and the contradictions of other men's lives lay in the outside world, and not in the fundamental nature of man himself. Just as most of his own errors and short-comings could be explained, he believed, by the influence of 'society', which had estranged him from his real nature, so did Rousseau also consider that man's alienation from himself and his failure to find spiritual fulfilment were the result of a fatal historical accident that had diverted him from his true destiny.

Since the ideal and original features of man's being went beyond the mere events and facts of history, its essential goodness had not been irretrievably impaired. Individual men might persecute the righteous and ruthless organizations might hound the innocent, but they could not destroy the spiritual basis of human existence. Rousseau considered this to be one of the most significant features of his own life. What he had found in his own heart was, in his opinion, part of the human heritage. If he attributed the exceptional elements of his own situation and character to the general decadence of the modern world rather than to any irremediable defect in human nature itself, it was because of his belief that the possibilities of his personal existence were relevant to the lives of his fellow men; he refused to separate the contemplation of his own ideal self from the vision of a regenerated humanity. Experience had taught him that perfect happiness was difficult to attain, but that it ought never to be rejected as impossible. The prospect of complete felicity through the achievement of unity, plenitude, and simplicity was constantly held before men's eyes as their right and privilege.

Rousseau's confidence in man's ability to fulfil what God and nature required of him and to achieve true happiness through his own freedom rather than divine grace made orthodox Christianity superfluous; revealed religion, in Rousseau's view, could add nothing distinctive to nature's gifts. Since it was man's natural goodness, not original sin, which constituted the essential truth of the human condition, Rousseau denied that revelation could bring anything but obscurity and confusion to spiritual problems. Jesus, in his opinion, was not the purveyor of grace, the unique intermediary between a transcendent God and fallen humanity, but simply the exceptional man of nature, unequalled, no doubt, in the history of the world, but in no sense a unique representative of supernatural spiritual power. From this point of view the orthodox were quite justified in treating Rousseau's religion as Pelagianism, since he allowed no room for original sin and the need for grace through Christ the Redeemer; man's natural goodness and freedom allowed him to achieve his own salvation. At the same time Rousseau's honest conviction that he was a true Christian revealed his reluctance or inability to set his own beliefs within the framework of a strictly theological outlook; he was convinced that he had found a spiritual attitude and an intuitive understanding of Jesus's teaching that went beyond the subtleties and distinctions of traditional theology.

Nevertheless, Rousseau's apparent rejection of 'revelation' and his indifference to theological distinctions, together with his aversion to all forms of social disorder, explain his curious conservatism in the matter of religious worship. After seeming to make Christianity either superfluous or harmful as a living spiritual force, he re-admitted it as a social institution, so that his challenging call for sincerity and honesty in the establishment of religious principles was accompanied by a great timidity in applying them to particular situations. In the absence of some kind of 'civil religion' based on essential moral principles, the ruler of the

State, in Rousseau's opinion, had the power and duty to determine the form of religious observance required of his subjects.

Rousseau saw no serious objection to this view because he believed that Christianity could not claim any absolute validity in its own right. Its value being directly dependent on its conformity with the principles of 'natural religion', it did not really matter (in Rousseau's eyes) which particular form of worship was adopted as the basis of the national cult; social rather than religious considerations ought to determine the matter. The stability and order of the State seemed to him more important than any question of particular religious 'truths'. In any case, he believed that it was only the essential principles of 'natural religion', not the particular dogmas of the Christian churches, that could claim the unqualified allegiance of all men.

The very qualities that gave value and meaning to Rousseau's religious outlook in the eyes of earlier generations may seem somewhat remote from the preoccupations of the modern world; most contemporary thinkers would perhaps prefer Kierkegaard's harsher portrayal of the spiritual condition of modern man to Rousseau's ultimately more optimistic and comforting picture. Seen in retrospect, Rousseau's religion appears much closer to the general eighteenth-century outlook than he himself was prepared to admit. The hostility of many Christians and *philosophes*, as well as his own feeling of personal isolation, led him to exaggerate the differences and overlook the similarities between his ideas and those of his contemporaries. The general cultural climate of his day was much more favourable to the eulogy of 'goodness' and 'nature' than to the condemnation of 'original sin'. As one writer has suggested, even the Christian Church itself, whether Roman Catholic or Protestant, contained leaders who were in many ways very close to Rousseau's views;[1] Molinists and rationalist Protestants were not far removed from his ideas about natural goodness and human freedom. Rousseau's own opposition to the philosophical materialism of thinkers like Diderot and Helvetius was apt to obscure his affinity with certain deistic beliefs which were indebted to nature rather than to revealed religion.

If many of Rousseau's religious ideas were less original than he himself believed, it still remains true that he brought to their expression the force and intensity of a complex personality fer-

[1] Cf. J. F. Thomas, *Le Pélagianisme de J.-J. Rousseau* (Paris, 1956).

vently attached to what for others were perhaps merely intellectual or conventional beliefs. As the preceding study has tried to show, to see Rousseau's philosophy of religion apart from the rest of his personality is to misunderstand its existential import. If Jean-Jacques exercised such a strong fascination upon contemporary and later Romantic generations, it was mainly because he made them aware of dormant powers, which, almost unknown to themselves, were beginning to thrust upwards to the light. The devotees of a rational culture were made conscious of the needs of their heart and imagination; the *Profession de foi* reminded men of the importance of their soul and conscience, whilst the *Contrat social* appealed to man's social sense by showing that sound political life could not exist without morality. Beyond the limitations and frustrations of everyday life Rousseau pointed to the possibility of a perfect world that completed instead of destroying man's most idealistic aspirations; the ideal and the real were shown to be two complementary aspects of the same fundamental experience. Consequently, ideas in danger of remaining abstract and lifeless began to glow with a new warmth and effulgence.

Yet, in another way, it is insufficient to affirm that Rousseau merely revitalized existing ideas, for it was impossible to do this without changing their essential character; the introduction of new personal elements into the interpretation of traditional concepts was bound to alter their ultimate meaning. Ideas imbued with the fervent spirit of a man like Rousseau inevitably irradiated beyond the intellectual horizon upon which his own gaze was so steadfastly fixed; his heart and his imagination added to his work a depth and intensity, the full implications of which he himself did not properly appreciate. In any case, he had always maintained that religious ideas could not remain mere concepts, but had to form part of a much fuller kind of experience. When once this experience was set in motion, it was difficult to foresee at what precise point it would stop, even though Jean-Jacques himself believed he understood the full implications of his outlook.

In his most buoyant moments Rousseau was confident that religious ideals had the power to refine the coarse texture of material existence and make it sensitive to the beauty of the 'ethereal regions'. At other times, however, he found the relationship between the finite and eternal aspects of existence less harmonious: in spite of his ardent spiritual aspirations, he could not prevent himself from being occasionally overwhelmed by a mood that seemed to threaten his most dearly-held convictions. Far from being satisfied with the quiet contemplation of perfection, he was apt to feel on such occasions that the ideal aspects of existence, however vivid and entrancing, remained a mere possibility rather than a real part of his everyday life. The bliss of 'earthly paradise' was disturbed by the intrusion of a feeling of frustration and emptiness and the awareness of an inexplicable inner 'void'. The infinite would suddenly appear as the negation and not the ecstatic fulfilment of immediate experience. If in certain moods the ideal could fascinate by the dream of possible perfection, it could at other times appal him by its lack of substance. Man, says Julie, is drawn on by his imagination and his desire to overcome the limitations of finite experience, but the object of his longing may be so elusive as to become a mere lack, a mere absence of satisfaction. Discontented with all that lies within his grasp and oppressed by the 'nothingness of human things', he may come to believe that, apart from God, 'there is nothing beautiful save what is not'; desire for perfection may be suddenly transformed into 'disgust' at present reality and the sterile longing of an empty heart for it knows not what. Similarly, the perfection of love may be inspired by a merely chimerical object and owe little or nothing to the real qualities of the loved person. Man's most complete moments of happiness on this earth are exposed to an inescapable feeling of *ennui*, which leaves him dissatisfied with all human pleasures. Thus, in spite of their close interdependence, the ideal and the real aspects of human existence may at times be in a state of irreconcilable antagonism.

Significantly enough, it was mainly in his personal and imaginative writings that Rousseau gave direct expression to this opposition between possibility and fulfilment, and even there the sense of emptiness was never completely separated from more positive feelings. The third letter to Malesherbes is typical of his general attitude. After describing his ecstatic enjoyment of nature and the imaginary world of perfect beings created 'after his own heart', he explains how this 'golden age' suddenly disappeared into 'an inexplicable void which nothing could have filled' and which left him acutely aware of the 'nothingness' of his dreams. Yet he immediately confesses that this feeling of emptiness had its euphoric aspect, for he felt himself lifted up by a 'heart-felt yearning' for some unknown, inconceivable form of enjoyment—a yearning that was itself enjoyment. Instead of abandoning himself to the feeling of nothingness, he at once let his thoughts rise up to 'all the beings of the world, the universal system of things, the incomprehensible being who encompasses everything'. His longing for the infinite thus ended in a mood of silent adoration before the majesty of God and the glories of his creation. Julie, too, admitted that the 'anxiety' of unsatisfied desire was a 'kind of enjoyment which made up for reality'; if she was so 'satiated' with happiness that she became the victim of an inescapable *ennui* that could be overcome only by death, death itself was finally envisaged not as the destruction of this earthly life but its completion in eternity. The infinite ideal appeared only temporarily as a darkening cloud; it soon revealed itself as the divine sun which shed its eternal light upon the dwellers in paradise.

Although certain elements in his personality and outlook, if given uninhibited expression, might have led to despair and anguish, Rousseau clung tenaciously and, as he supposed, triumphantly to his ideal of a unified existence. Even his belief in immortality was largely sustained by the hope that the next world would bring him the plenitude of a perfect fulfilment that could be glimpsed only fleetingly in this. Freedom was a positive good; if it opened up the possibility of nothingness, it was only to overcome it through a higher form of being. The infinite dimension of existence was ultimately deemed to be consoling and beneficial in its effect, for even the most wretched man—and did not Rousseau himself believe in the uniqueness of his own iniquitous position as a good and innocent man persecuted by a hostile world?—could confidently look forward to perfect bliss in the after-life.

For a later thinker like Kierkegaard, on the other hand, victory could not be so easily won. He held up Rousseau as 'an example of what it means not to be well read in Christianity'.[1] Jean-Jacques, he insisted, had failed to understand the true nature of 'Christian conflict'. In Kierkegaard's view, freedom was not a merely comforting aspect of human existence, for it was bound up with man's awareness of himself as a sinful creature separated by a 'yawning

---

[1] *The Journals of Søren Kierkegaard*, edited and translated by A. Dru (Oxford, 1938), Entries 1204–5. The question is discussed more fully in the chapter on 'Kierkegaard and Rousseau' in my *Søren Kierkegaard and French Literature* (Cardiff, 1966).

gap' from God's absolute transcendence. Salvation could not come from a confident acceptance of man's natural goodness, but only through a 'leap' into faith—a leap made in 'fear and trembling' and with the 'dreadful' awareness of its uncertainty. Instead of relying on nature or reason to resolve the anguishing possibilities of existence, man had to abandon himself to the paradox of faith in Christ the God-Man and the eventual outpouring of divine grace.

A purely personal opinion that Kierkegaard was a greater religious thinker than Rousseau is largely irrelevant to a study that has been concerned almost entirely with description and analysis—with deciding what a particular man's religion was, rather than what it is worth. No doubt it would be quite contrary to the spirit of Rousseau's religious outlook to refuse to take sides in a debate involving the all-important question of man's destiny on this earth, but he believed this to be a matter which each individual had to decide for himself as sincerely as he could. Perhaps Jean-Jacques rather too readily assumed that because 'reason is common to all men' and all have the same 'interest' in heeding its voice, all men of good faith would eventually think like him. Even so, he never sought to persuade others to adopt views which he himself did not fervently believe, and he exhorted his readers to accept only those ideas to which they could respond 'in the simplicity of their hearts'. His whole enterprise thus serves to remind believers and unbelievers alike of every man's need to ensure, at least once in his life, that what he outwardly professes he inwardly believes with his entire being. It may then emerge that 'religion' is not such an easy matter as many at first suppose and that—if we may adapt some words of Montaigne once quoted by Jean-Jacques himself—each is richer—or poorer—than he thinks.

BIBLIOGRAPHY

A. Rousseau's Works:

Œuvres complètes de Jean-Jacques Rousseau, edited by B. Gagnebin and M. Raymond, Bibliothèque de la Pléiade (Paris, 1959–).

Œuvres complètes de J.-J. Rousseau, 13 vols. (Hachette, Paris, 1865–70, etc.).

Œuvres et correspondance inédites de J. J. Rousseau, ed. G. Streckeisen Moultou (Paris, 1861).

Correspondance complète de Jean-Jacques Rousseau, ed. by R. A. Leigh, Vols. I–IV (Geneva, 1965–).

Correspondance générale de Jean-Jacques Rousseau, ed. T. Dufour and P. P. Plan, 20 vols. (Paris, 1924–34).

Lettre à M. d'Alembert sur les spectacles, ed. M. Fuchs (Geneva, 1948).

La Profession de foi du Vicaire Savoyard, ed. P.-M. Masson (Paris–Fribourg, 1914).

La Profession de foi du Vicaire savoyard, ed. G. Beaulavon (Paris, 1937).

Annales de la Société Jean-Jacques Rousseau, Geneva 1905–, also contain hitherto unpublished material.

B. Secondary Sources:

Of the many works about Rousseau the following are especially relevant to the theme of the present study.

AMIEL, H. F., in *Rousseau jugé par les Genevois d'aujourd'hui* (Geneva, 1879).

BROOME, J. H., *Rousseau: A Study of his Thought* (London, 1963).

BURGELIN, P., *La Philosophie de l'existence de J.-J. Rousseau* (Paris, 1952).

BURGELIN, P., *Jean-Jacques Rousseau et la religion de Genève* (Geneva, 1962).

CASSIRER, E., *The Question of Jean-Jacques Rousseau*, trans. P. Gay (New York, 1962).

DERATHÉ, R., *Le Rationalisme de Rousseau* (Paris, 1948).

DERATHÉ, R., 'Jean-Jacques Rousseau et le Christianisme', in *Revue de Métaphysique et de Morale*, LIII (1948), pp. 379–414.
EIGELDINGER, M., *Jean-Jacques Rousseau et la réalite de l'imaginaire* (Paris, 1964).
FABRE, J. (ed.), *Jean-Jacques Rousseau et son œuvre* (Neuchâtel 1962).
GREEN, F. C., *Jean-Jacques Rousseau* (Cambridge, 1955).
GRIMSLEY, R., *Jean-Jacques Rousseau, a Study in Self-Awareness* (Cardiff, 1961).
GUÉHENNO, J., *Jean-Jacques*, 3 vols. (Paris, 1940–52). New edition in 2 vols. entitled *Jean-Jacques, Histoire d'une conscience* (1962). English translation entitled *Jean-Jacques Rousseau*, by J. and D. Weightman, 2 vols. (London, 1966).
HENDEL, C. W., *Jean-Jacques Rousseau, Moralist*, 2 vols. (New York, O.U.P., 1934).
MASSON, P.-M., *La Religion de J.-J. Rousseau*, 3 vols. (Paris, 1916).
MUNTEANO, B., 'La Solitude de Rousseau', in *Annales Jean-Jacques Rousseau*, XXXI (1946–9), pp. 79–168.
POULET, G. *Études sur le temps humain* (Paris, 1950).
RAYMOND, M., *J.-J. Rousseau: La Quête de soi et la rêverie* (Paris, 1962).
SAINT-PIERRE, B. de, *La vie et les ouvrages de J.-J. Rousseau*, ed. M. Souriau (Paris, 1907).
SCHINZ, A., *La Pensée de Jean-Jacques Rousseau* (Paris, 1962).
SCHINZ, A., *La Pensée religieuse de J.-J. Rousseau et ses récents interprètes* (Paris, 1927).
SPINK, J. S., *Rousseau et Genève* (Paris, 1934).
STAROBINSKI, J., *Jean-Jacques Rousseau, la transparence et l'obstacle* (Paris, 1957).
THOMAS, J. F., *Le Pélagianisme de Jean-Jacques Rousseau* (Paris, 1956).
VALLETTE, G., *Jean-Jacques Rousseau genevois* (Paris, 1908).
WRIGHT, E. H., *The Meaning of Rousseau* (Oxford, 1929).

INDEX

d'Alembert, 2, 19, 52, 78n.
Amiel, 95, 143
amour de soi, amour-propre, 39, 62, 66, 69, 124, 134
atheism, 21, 23, 33, 54, 86

Beaulavon, G., 53
beauty, 8, 50, 52, 57, 93-94, 101, 129, 134, 139
Berkeley, 52
Bernard, Abraham, 3-4, 98
Bernard, Gabriel, 4
Bernard, Jacques, 1
Bernard, Suzanne, 1
Bible, 2, 19, 25, 30, 72, 121
Bomston, Lord, 44, 117
books, 70
Boothby, Brooke, 32
botany, 28
Broome, J. H., 143
Burgelin, P., xiin., 73n., 79, 84n., 133n., 143

Calvin, 79
Calvinism, 1, 5
Cassirer, E., 143
'chain of beings', 55
childhood, 14, 96-98, 109
children, Rousseau's, 13, 20
Christianity, 3, 13, 39, 47, 69, 77, 79, 83f., 137-8
civilization, 1, 49, 61, 66, 130
Clarke, Samuel, 11, 46, 50
Columbus, 104
Condillac, 32, 52
Confessions, 3, 4, 5, 9, 12, 21, 26, 45, 67, 96, 101, 102, 103, 109, 124, 132
conscience, 9, 61, 70, 71, 73, 77, 133
contemplation, 17, 54, 60, 68, 88, 118f., 125, 129, 140
Contrat social, i, 3, 27, 49, 79, 84, 139
Crocker, L. G., 121n.
Crousaz, 56
Crusoe, 29, 104

Death, 57, 97
De l'Esprit (Helvétius), 58
Derathé, R., 46n., 47n., 50, 69n., 143, 144
Descartes, 44, 53, 54
destiny, 31-32, 125-7, 136
Dialogues, 32, 73, 90, 101, 102, 106, 118, 119, 124, 125-7
Diderot, 13, 19, 21, 52, 55, 138
Discours sur les Sciences et les Arts, 37, 42
Discours sur l'Inégalité, 16, 57, 59, 66, 96
doubt, 22-23, 40, 81
Ducommun, Abel, 5
Dufour, T., 7n.
Du Peyrou, 31n.

Ecclesiastes, 30
Eigeldinger, M., 95n., 144
Émile, i, 22, 24, 25-26, 49, 50n., 63, 80, 84, 92
ennui, 9, 112, 140
Entretiens sur les Sciences (Lamy), 10
d'Épinay, Mme., 17
Essay on Man (Pope), 11, 13
eternity, 8, 33, 93
evil, 9, 17, 56, 64, 109, 124f.
existence, 18, 29, 52, 65, 87, 90, 96, 130, 134

Fabre, J., 144
fatality. *See* destiny
father-theme, 108, 113f., 129
feeling, 7, 29, 47-8, 50, 53, 58, 62, 64, 71. *See also* 'heart'
felicity, i, 8, 33, 66, 67, 87, 94, 99, 116, 119, 128
Fénelon, 68
fire-symbol, 107
Franquières. *See* Letter to Franquières
freedom, 13, 24, 49, 60, 64, 121, 134, 137, 141

Gaime, abbé, 8

INDEX

Galley, Mlle., 92n.
Gâtier, abbé, 8
Geneva, 1–5, 8, 14–16, 17, 27
Gessner, 25
Gilliard, E., 102n.
God, 14, 24, 29, 31, 32, 34, 54f., 93, 106, 107f., 133
goodness, 31, 46, 51, 56, 64, 69, 94, 113–15, 123, 126, 129, 136–7
Gospels, 71, 74, 83, 85
grace, 137, 142
Graffenried, Mlle de, 92n.
Green, F. C., 12, 35, 144
Grimm, 19
Grimsley, R., 20n., 33n., 52n., 141n., 144
Grotius, 16
Guéhenno, J., 2
guilt, 9, 20, 99, 110, 125
Guyon, B., 111n.

Happiness, 3, 7, 8, 21, 24, 29, 33, 66, 93, 122, 129, 130. *See also* felicity
heart, xii, 48, 61, 71, 101, 131, 133, 139
hell, 123f.
Helvétius, 58, 138
Hendel, C. W., 44n., 144
history, 71–72, 131
d'Holbach, 13
d'Houdetot, Mme., 19, 21, 98

Idylles, (Gessner), 25
imagination, xiii, 44, 89, 94, 99, 106, 124, 139, 140
Imitation of Jesus Christ, 30
immortality, 11, 33, 34, 60, 66, 67, 90, 97, 141
Incarnation, 32, 76
inner life, 10, 11, 14, 20, 21, 23, 29, 42, 45, 54, 58f.
innocence, 7–8, 15, 24, 25, 31, 90f., 103, 110, 113–14, 118, 121–2, 124, 128, 136
intelligence, 11, 56
'interest', 10, 42, 50, 51, 52–53, 59, 63, 69, 76, 133, 135, 142
Isaiah, 30
Islam, 77
island-theme, 95, 111, 118, 129
d'Ivernois, 28

Jansenism, 9
Jeremiah, 30
Jesuits, 12, 24
Jesus, 31, 72f., 80, 137
Jews, 72
Job, 30
Judaism, 77
judgement, 53, 59, 60
Julie, xiii, 21, 47, 48, 54, 91, 98, 107, 108, 109f., 120, 128, 140
justice, 31, 53, 62

Kempis, T. à, 30
Kierkegaard, 41, 43, 80, 138, 141

Lambercier, 3, 109
Lamy, B., 10
language, ix–x, 30, 90, 119
Leibniz, 18, 56
Leigh, R. A., 143
Lemaître de Claville, 11
Levasseur, Thérèse, 13, 19, 20, 35
Luxembourg, Maréchal de, 20
Luxembourg, Maréchale de, 20
Letter on Providence, 55–6, 58, 65
Letter to Franquières, 30, 36, 38, 40, 46
Lettre à d'Alembert, 19, 24, 78n., 122–3
Lettre à Beaumont, 26, 37, 39, 41
Lettres à Malesherbes, 92, 93, 105, 106, 140
Lettres écrites de la Campagne, 27
Lettres écrites de la Montagne, 27, 73, 74f., 78
Lettres morales, 21, 24, 42, 48
Lévite d'Éphraïm, Le, 25
Locke, 52, 86
look, the, 33, 108f., 114, 118, 122, 128
love, 97

Malesherbes, 25. See also *Lettres à Malesherbes*
man, primitive, x, 57, 66, 96, 118
Masson, P.–M., xi, 2, 5, 10, 11, 13, 15, 30n., 31, 55, 144
materialism, 54–55, 61, 135, 163
metaphysics, 36, 45, 134
miracles, 74f.
Molinism, 138
Montaigne, 45, 61, 142
Montmollin, 25f.

INDEX

Moses, 75
mother-theme, 29, 102, 108, 113, 129
movement, 55
Munteano, B., 91n., 105n., 144n.
music, 12, 122
mythology, xiii–xiv, 87f.

Naomi, 121
nature, 6–7, 16–17, 28–29, 31, 35, 39, 45, 47–48, 52, 56, 57, 60, 61, 63, 70, 71, 89–90, 92, 100f., 108, 129, 130, 137
Nouvelle Héloïse, La, xiii, 14, 19, 21, 24, 36, 44, 46, 54, 103, 105, 107f., 123–5

d'Offreville, 63
opinion, 39, 63, 70, 130, 131
order, 18, 48, 50n., 59, 63, 66, 67, 94, 115, 129, 134

Paradise, xiv, 3, 7, 24, 87f., 112, 140
patriotism, 15, 83f.
Paul, St., 73
Pelagianism, 137
perfection, 44, 54, 87, 94, 132, 139, 140
philosophy, xi–xii, 15, 36f.
Plato, 44n., 46, 86, 132
Pluche, 10
Plutarch, 16, 117
Pope, A., 11, 13, 18, 55, 56
Poulet, G., 144
pragmatism, 51
prayer, 7, 29
Profession de foi, xiv, 11, 21, 24, 26, 31, 34, 36, 39, 47, 51, 54, 58, 61, 71, 73, 139
Protestantism, 3, 15, 25f., 77f., 138
Providence, 18, 31–32, 35, 58, 65, 126
punishment, eternal, 10, 123
purity, 7, 8, 15, 103, 118

Quinault, Mlle., 14

Rachel, 121
Ramsay, Allan, 125
rationalism, 46, 71
Raymond, M., 91, 105
reason, x, xii, 19, 46f., 53, 61, 62, 65, 70, 73, 77, 133, 142
rebirth, 91, 117

reflection, i, 18, 39, 63, 96, 130, 133
Reformation, 79
religion, civil, 3, 84, 137
religion, natural, 8, 34, 68f., 131, 138
revelation, 11, 68f., 137
reverie, 66, 87–88, 93, 101, 103
Rêveries du Promeneur solitaire, 22, 29, 30, 90, 105
Roman Catholicism, 3, 5, 6, 11, 12, 26f., 77f., 138
Rousseau, Isaac, 1, 16
Ruth, 121

Saint-Aubin, 11
Saint-Pierre, Abbé de, 83
Saint-Pierre, B. de, 30, 144
Saint-Preux, xiii, 38, 39, 44, 98, 99, 100, 105, 107, 110, 114, 116f., 128
Schinz, A., 144
self-sufficiency, 4, 12, 29, 34, 93, 96, 98–99, 113, 129
sensation, 51, 52, 59, 60
Sermon on the Mount, 30
sex, 97
signs, 31–33, 119–20, 125
simplicity, 3, 25, 44, 46, 64, 69, 71, 92, 121, 135
sin, original, 64, 80, 137
sincerity, 41f., 81, 132–3n.
society, 3, 14, 22–23, 37, 39, 42, 62, 64, 70, 76f., 90, 131, 136
Socinianism, 2
Socrates, 72–73
Solitaires, Les, 91
Spectacle de la Nature, (Pluche), 10
Spink, J. S., 144
Starobinski, J., xiin., 92, 100, 111n., 120, 121, 144
State, Church and, 83f.
sublimity, 50, 62, 64, 71, 88, 93, 101, 117, 118
subtlety, 37, 58, 64, 69, 76, 92, 130, 133, 135, 137
Sur la loi naturelle, (Voltaire), 18
Sur le désastre de Lisbonne, (Voltaire), 18

Tacitus, 16
Thomas, J. F., 138n., 144
time, 8, 93
tolerance, 19, 85

Traité de l'opinion, (Saint-Aubin), 11
Traité du vrai mérite, (Claville), 11
transparence, 118, 126
Tronchin, J. R., 27
truth, 32, 37, 41, 51–53, 58, 131–3, 135
Turgot, 52
Turrettini, J. A., 1

Vallette, G., 2n., 144
Vernes, J., 14

Vernet, J., 1
virtue, 10, 13, 14, 33, 37, 49, 50, 53, 60, 61, 64, 115
Vision de Pierre de la Montagne, 28
Voltaire, 17f., 36, 37, 55, 56, 58, 65, 84

Warens, Mme de, 5f., 88, 90, 99, 109
water-theme, 102
Wolmar, 21, 109, 114, 120, 128
will, 55, 59
Wright, E. H., 144